The Woman's Fix-It Guide to
Kitchen Makeovers

The Woman's Fix-It Guide to
Kitchen Makeovers

by Karen Dale Dustman

Illustrated by Cindi Dixon and Eva Stina Bender

CHANDLER HOUSE PRESS
Worcester, MA

THE WOMAN'S FIX-IT GUIDE TO KITCHEN MAKEOVERS

ISBN 1-886284-49-0
Library of Congress Card Number: 99-069796
First Edition
ABCDEFGHIJK

Published by
Chandler House Press
335 Chandler Street
Worcester, MA 01602
USA

President
Lawrence J. Abramoff

Director of Publishing
Claire Cousineau

Editorial/Production Manager
James A. Karis II

Book Design
Michele Italiano-Perla

Cover Design
Will Ragano

Illustrations
Cindi Dixon and Eva Stina Bender

Chandler House Press books are available at special discounts for bulk purchases. For more information about how to arrange such purchases, please contact Chandler House Press, 335 Chandler Street, Worcester, MA 01602, or call (800) 642-6657, or fax (508) 756-9425, or find us on the World Wide Web at www.chandlerhousepress.com.

Chandler House Press books are distributed to the trade by
National Book Network, Inc.
4720 Boston Way
Lanham, MD 20706
(800) 462-6420

DISCLAIMER:

This book is intended to provide a general introduction to common remodeling topics and materials, but of course it cannot offer definitive advice about all situations. There is no substitute for competent, in-person professional assistance.

We also don't presume to advise you about local building codes, which vary considerably across the nation. Always consult your local building department for guidance before beginning any remodeling or home improvement project. In some cases, you may be required to obtain a permit before the work begins, and inspections may be necessary as you proceed.

One final word about risk and responsibility: there's danger everywhere in life these days. A task as simple as crossing the street has pitfalls! Certainly some of the projects discussed in this book may involve an element of potential risk (from lead paint or tipping ladders, for example). We've tried to flag areas where a precautionary step may be in order. However, the author and the publisher cannot and do not assume responsibility for any damage, harm or injury caused by or related to any remodeling efforts or techniques described in this book.

If you have any questions, we strongly advise you to call in a licensed professional. Take care, and work safely!

Acknowledgments

So many wonderful folks contributed in one way or another to this book that it's hard to say thank you enough! Still, I want to extend my heartfelt thanks and appreciation:

To B. Smith, for her kind help and warm spirit.

To Rose Levy Beranbaum, Marie Cappuccio, Ann Cooper, Cindi Dixon, Meredith Gould, Helen Jay, Michael Lamb, Jane Langmuir, Lesley Morrison, Michael Pantano, Ann Potter, Lisa Schroeder, Joan Stanford, and most especially, culinary legend Julia Child, for generously contributing their witty, wise and wonderful "Tips From The Pros."

To Cindi Dixon and Eva Bender, whose beautiful illustrations for this book share a glimpse of their beautiful spirits.

To all those gracious folks who reviewed drafts and kindly offered advice and suggestions, including Cullen Hackler of the Porcelain Enamel Institute; Michael Lamb of EREC; architect par excellence Leon Gogain; financial whiz Jim Brown; ever-patient Dick Dustman; and the folks at the Lead Information Hotline (any errors remaining despite their efforts, of course, being solely my own!).

To friend extraordinaire Cindy Miller, who is utterly unafraid of tackling any home-improvement project and has gone the last mile for me so many times—including reorganizing my kitchen.

And to my husband Rick, without whom none of this would have been written.

Contents

Foreword

The kitchen, they say, is the heart of the home. And it's easy to see why! The kitchen is the perfect spot to snuggle up with a cup of hot chocolate as you wait out a winter storm, or to find a cooling splash of iced tea to beat that summertime heat.

Some of my fondest childhood memories were set in the kitchen of our Pennsylvania home, where my mother, grandmother, and three aunts would whip up fabulous fare for gala picnics and holiday dinners, somber funerals and festive weddings. Even as a child, the kitchen was where I could always count on finding good friends, good company, good conversation and, of course, great food!

But what woman hasn't wished she could perk up her kitchen a little—increase the storage space, add better lighting, improve the appliances or just update the color scheme?

Here's a book that can help make all that possible. With a dash of humor and plenty of plain common sense, author Karen Dale Dustman takes you through the process, from deciding what to change to making sure the final product is exactly right—and, of course, right on budget. Whether you're a do-it-yourselfer or prefer to let your checkbook do the work, *The Woman's Fix-It Guide to Kitchen Makeovers* can help you create the kitchen "with style" you've always wanted—and the perfect place for creating tomorrow's memories!

—*B. Smith*

Restaurateur, author of *B. Smith's Entertaining and Cooking for Friends*, and *B. Smith: Rituals and Celebrations*, lifestyle expert, host of the nationally syndicated TV show "B. Smith With Style," editor-in-chief of *B. Smith Style* magazine

Introduction

There's no room in the house that says "home" quite like a kitchen. It's the place where you grab your first cup of coffee every morning, snag a cookie or two as you come home, and savor a glass of milk before bedtime. It's no wonder they call the kitchen the heart of the home—but it's also the room most women seem to want to change!

A recent survey by home improvement giant Owens Corning shows that 29 percent of the women surveyed would like to remodel their kitchen and/or bath in the next five years. Why? Styles change. Cooking options and materials change. And let's face it—women's tastes change.

But you don't have to live with yesterday's kitchen. This book will help you pinpoint exactly what to include in an efficient remodel—and even help you do some of the work yourself, if you're so inclined. Always hated that counter area where the light never seems to reach? Watch your work space sparkle with a new window, under-cabinet lighting, and perhaps even new solid-surfacing top! Can't stand your dated cabinets or dingy linoleum? Ring in the millennium with a whole new look!

Because not every homeowner has the same needs—or budget—we've broken this book up into easy-to-use sections. Check out "Little Things That Make a Difference" for quick, easy, and nearly-painless-on-the-checkbook ways to add a dash of color and a big dollop of convenience.

"Facelifts on a Budget" takes the process one step further, with upgrades like cabinet faces and linoleum flooring that can make a big difference for a relatively modest price.

"Lighting Options" and "Fixtures With Splash" help you make the most of your existing layout with new windows, lighting, and appliances, while "Small-Space Solutions" is just that—ways to wangle extra space, create a baking center, and end cookbook clutter.

And finally, for those fortunate enough to have a more generous budget in mind, we dive into "All-Out Excitement!" with tips for rearranging your entire layout and choosing among today's exciting new countertop and cabinet options.

Planning, of course, is the key to success in any remodeling project—and that's especially true when it comes to as complex an ecosystem as your kitchen. Not only do you need to select an attractive blend of colors, styles and materials, but the end result has to promote efficient work patterns and traffic flow as well.

To guide you through the maze of choices, we've included handy "Tips" boxes as we go along. We've flagged various perils and pitfalls to alert you to some of the most common remodelers' woes. And for further questions or more extensive help, we've included a reference list in the appendix with manufacturers' toll-free hotlines, a handy guide to standard kitchen dimensions, and various other helpful sources of information.

Perhaps best of all, you'll discover a terrific assortment of "Tips From the Pros" sprinkled throughout the text. We gleaned these creative suggestions from some of America's most kitchen-savvy folks—from professional chefs to professional organizers! You'll meet each of them, at least briefly, in the "Biographies" pages at the end.

Any remodeling project, of course, can present a few challenges. You've probably heard at least one horror story or two (and if you haven't already seen it, I'd recommend renting "The Money Pit" before you begin). But remodeling can also be a glorious opportunity to sweep out the old, and watch exciting new dreams materialize.

Ready to get started? Grab a few pencils, put your imagination in gear, and let's go!

Planning: It's A Family Affair!

Wʜat's hot and what's not in kitchen design has changed a bit over the years. My grandmother's farmhouse kitchen, "modernized" in the rural electrification push of the 1930s, boasted a solitary light bulb dangling by its wires in the center of the room. And before electric refrigerators became the norm, families typically made do with a drippy icebox relegated to an eminently practical (though not exactly convenient) position on a service porch.

The postwar building boom of the '40s and '50s spelled the end for cramped, dark kitchen quarters. "I Love Lucy"-era dream kitchens boasted such innovations as a built-in breakfast nook or a gleaming, chrome-accented dinette. Technology had a hand in revamping kitchen expectations, too. During the '60s and '70s, the "modern" kitchen came to include such *de rigueur* innovations as a built-in dishwasher, garbage disposal, and perhaps a trash compactor. And by the '80s, even the walls were pushed boldly outward as the kitchen stretched form and function yet again in its new incarnation as "great room."

Today just as surely as in yesteryear, the kitchen remains the hub of everyday life. But *how* we live, work, and eat is changing. And kitchens are changing in response.

Hectic, on-the-go lifestyles mean Americans eat more meals away from home, and depend more on "convenience" foods such as packaged mixes and pre-cleaned vegetables

Are Grandma's cooking skills fast becoming a lost art? One research firm's rather depressing prediction: By the year 2005, many Americans will never have prepared an entire meal from scratch!

—Source: The McKinsey Quarterly, 1996, Number 4

TIPS FROM THE PROS:

"My kitchen sink is a relic salvaged from the old fire station in my hometown. It's a beautiful, HUGE, old porcelain sink, and every time I run water in this sink I love it. Maybe it's using a light fixture from a home you used to live in; maybe it's a vase handed down from your grandmother. But I think it's important to incorporate something in your kitchen that makes it uniquely ... YOURS."

—*Cindi Dixon, illustrator and photographer*

when they *do* cook at home. Despite the proliferation of those mouth-watering gourmet cooking shows on television, the operative words for much of American cooking in practice seem to be "fast" and "simple."

Today's kitchens need to simplify meal preparation, facilitate cleanup chores, and perhaps double as family room and home office. With all we expect of a kitchen, it's no wonder that the kitchen is one of the most popular remodeling targets. And luckily, a kitchen remodeling can be one of the most cost-effective upgrades to your home. Just how much of the expense you can expect to recover in value added to your home depends on the changes you make and where you live, but recent estimates by *Remodeling* magazine suggest that, on average, homeowners can expect to recoup between 94 and 102 percent of their outlay for a minor kitchen makeover, and about 90 percent of the cost of a major kitchen remodeling project.

Taking A Closer Look

Before you draw a single wishful line, take a moment to evaluate exactly what you have. Does your kitchen boast vintage hardware or original crown moldings? Do you have a charming antique stove or other appliance you'd like to show off? Are you happy with the existing storage and counter space, or dying for a little extra elbowroom? How efficient is your current layout? What are its limitations?

Then try to be realistic about what you really NEED. What kind of cooking do you do—baking, barbecuing, quick leftovers reheating? Do you do any formal entertaining? Think not just about what you need today, but five or even ten years down the line. Will you be selling? Retiring? Have kids who will be leaving home—or perhaps expect more kids on the way? Is there a chance you might need to accommodate the special needs of elders? Or are you getting older yourself?

If you have pets, don't forget to include them in your planning. Will you need a spot for doggie dishes, a pet door for your favorite feline, or a niche for a birdcage?

Think also about what you can do WITHOUT. Do you really use that built-in double oven that came with your home? Would you really be heartbroken if your new kitchen didn't include a trash compactor—or a computer? Are there compromises or trade-offs you'd be willing to make on materials if it helped keep costs down?

Bottom line: Like most other things in life, you'll be happiest with the end result if you've really thought things through ahead of time. I'm a firm believer that practical IS beautiful—when in doubt, choose items that will last and are designed for ease of use over awkward but trendy alternatives.

Whatever your ultimate wish list, it will probably need to be balanced by budget concerns. But try not to scrimp when it comes to what you want most. If you can't afford to upgrade your entire kitchen now, consider tackling the project in stages.

TIPS FROM THE PROS:

"In many ways, I find a small workspace really works best. Believe it or not, in my home the kitchen is very small. When you plan on a big kitchen, you start out thinking 'anything goes' and then find you're forced to take ten steps to the stove, and twenty to the refrigerator. You shouldn't have to walk a mile to prepare dinner; ideally, everything should be within arm's reach, or just a couple of steps away. Ask yourself how big a kitchen you really NEED. It's probably smaller than you think."

—Lisa Schroeder, executive chef and owner, Mother's Bistro & Bar

Just Your Style

When you think of the needs you want YOUR new kitchen to serve, be sure you consider more than just basic cooking and cleanup chores. Think style and lifestyle as well!

> **Is your home in a historic district? In addition to your other planning, remember that you may need to meet requirements of an architectural review committee.**

- Do you share cooking duties? How many people will need to be able to move around in the kitchen at one time?
- Would you like a special serving area for entertaining, or to accommodate a large family?
- Do you do a lot of one type of cooking (baking, grilling, barbecuing, microwave cooking)?
- Do you need a place for kids to do homework? For hobbies? A home office?
- What sorts of appliances are on your wish list—from functional to pure entertainment (such as a TV)?
- What's your decorating style? Are you an inveterate knickknack collector or a "raw simplicity" vacant-countertop type?
- What overall FEELING do you want your kitchen to convey? Homey and comfortable? Fun and funky? Refined and elegant?
- Where will you put pet food dishes? Is a doggie door important?
- Do you make lavish use of cut flowers or potted plants? How can you easily handle watering chores?
- Do you want to investigate "green" eco-friendly material choices?

Low Impact Living

Today, it's more practical than ever to include "green" options as you design your new kitchen! You probably already know what a big "bottom-line" difference energy-efficient windows, light fixtures, and appliances can make in your utility bills—and ultimately, for the planet. Here are a few other earth-friendly ideas you may want to consider in your kitchen planning:

- ✎ Install a ceiling fan to help distribute warmer air in winter, and provide cooling breezes in summertime.
- ✎ Look for materials with natural or recycled-material components (cork flooring; tile that uses salvaged marble chips; countertop materials that include recycled glass; cabinets made without formaldehyde; lumber that's certified as being harvested using sound forestry-management practices, rather than clear-cutting).
- ✎ Include a spot for recycling containers in your kitchen design.
- ✎ Choose nontoxic or less toxic paints and sealers; use biodegradable strippers.
- ✎ If you're planning major renovations, check out cellulose insulation materials made with recycled newspaper.
- ✎ "Recycle" as much as you can from your existing kitchen (reuse existing cabinets and appliances, for example), or check out the fascinating choices at a building material salvage outlet. (Weigh the savings of more energy-efficient appliances, however. Reuse appliances only if they're still in good condition and if dimensions are standard, so future replacement won't be jinxed!)

Note: To help you locate "eco-friendly" options, we've listed contact information for a variety of sources in the "Sources & Resources" appendix at the back of this book.

TIPS FROM THE PROS:

"Unless you are totally cyber-dependent, have a network system in your home, and will go through withdrawal agonies without a computer monitor in your kitchen, stick to old-fashioned recipe cards. They're handy, user-friendly, and really, aren't you charmed every time you see Aunt Matty's handwriting and those splatters of meals gone by?"

—*Meredith Gould, author of Working at Home*

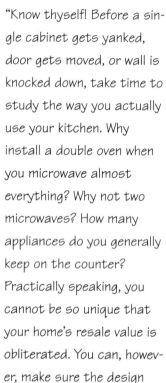

TIPS FROM THE PROS:

"Know thyself! Before a single cabinet gets yanked, door gets moved, or wall is knocked down, take time to study the way you actually use your kitchen. Why install a double oven when you microwave almost everything? Why not two microwaves? How many appliances do you generally keep on the counter? Practically speaking, you cannot be so unique that your home's resale value is obliterated. You can, however, make sure the design reflects your workflow, traffic patterns, and cooking preferences. Now is your chance to have it your way. Pretty much."

—Meredith Gould, author of *Working at Home*

Dreaming & Scheming

So, where do you start? One of the most *fun* parts of any remodeling job is the "dreaming and scheming" stage. And remember, you don't have to dream from scratch. Clip magazine photos that grab your imagination; stop by a kitchen showroom—or three. Grill your friends about what they've loved (and hated) in their own kitchens. Collect manufacturers' brochures to compare the latest and greatest in what's available. New cabinet designs, for example, now offer options like a built-in breadbox, under-cabinet stem glass rack, and even a pullout ironing board.

Model homes can be another great source of inspiration. They'll all look great, of course—those new home decorators work hard to make that brand-new house look, well, "homey." So remember to look past the superficial flash as you're scouting for serious design elements.

If you're angling for historical accuracy—or if you just happened to fall in love with a particular "vintage" look—you may be able to find a wealth of information on period-appropriate colors, designs, and styles through your local historical society. Museums and "living history" sites such as Williamsburg, Virginia, can also be excellent

sources of historically accurate detail. Don't overlook your local library—architecture and design books may contain helpful photos and suggestions. Some paint stores now offer free color charts to help you duplicate historical color combinations.

For now, at least, give yourself permission to "think outside the box." What would your kitchen look like if money were no object? If you dared to use spring-flower colors? If your child designed it herself?

Planning is the MOST important part of a remodeling, so DON'T BE IN A HURRY. Give yourself plenty of time in the "scheming and dreaming" stage. Plans that "age" for a few months tend to be more complete. Remember, information is cheap; changing your mind in the middle of remodeling is most likely going to be costly.

Creative Collaborating

Your husband or significant other will probably have plenty of opinions on the remodeling process (and if he's like mine, won't hesitate to share 'em!). But it can also be fun to involve your kids in the project.

You might ask each child to pick a favorite crayon color, and see if there's a way to incorporate those hues in your kitchen color scheme. Or if "midnight black" is the childhood choice du jour, try offering two or three more reasonable shades from paint chips, and put the final decision to a family vote.

Would your kids enjoy having their own kitchen work area? Consider designing a special, shorter, counter section or table, just for them. Are your preteens fanatical movie-and-popcorn fans? Make sure the microwave oven will be located where they can safely reach it.

TIP

Just as you bring a magazine photo of a haircut you like to your stylist, a picture may be worth a thousand words in communicating with your contractor. Consider starting a series of folders or envelopes to help you organize clippings and photos by subject— appliances, lighting, cabinets, paint colors, etc.

Don't forget to take plenty of "before" pictures before you begin.

TIP:

If you plan on selling your home in the next three to five years, talk with a reputable real estate agent about what kitchen features are hot selling points in your neighborhood, and what changes could help make your home more marketable. An experienced agent can also provide valuable feedback about whether you might be going overboard on your budget, and will alert you if they feel you're choosing offbeat colors or styles that could hinder a future sale.

I confess to misgivings about anything that smacks of management-by-committee—particularly when it comes to something quite as personal as my kitchen. But some truly adventuresome women have tackled remodeling tasks with "a little help from their friends," making it a festive GROUP project.

If you're not sure you trust your friends' taste and talents quite that far, consider at least sharing your success when it's over in a round-robin of toasts and tales. One woman I know organized a celebratory "dinner on the go" with five other women who'd recently undertaken home-improvement projects on their own. After hors d'oeuvres at one house, where they admired a fireplace hearth the host had just installed herself, the group crossed the street for a main dish in a second woman's newly tiled kitchen, then shared dessert and compliments across town, where they admired yet another woman's newly finished paint job. Now, that's creative!

How To Budget—*Without Breaking The Bank!*

Once you start pricing the elements of a kitchen remodeling, you'll quickly see how easy it is to run up a bill roughly the size of the national debt. But how much should you spend? The oft-repeated rule of thumb is that unless you're planning to stay put for at least another ten years, you should limit your expected outlay to no more than 15 percent of your home's current value.

It's easy enough to add up the prices of appliances, flooring, and countertops—and if you decide to use a contractor, you'll have (or should have) a firm bid in writing. But remember that you'll need to budget for some easy-to-overlook "ups and extras" as well. Be sure you factor in sales tax and delivery charges. Depending on the scope of your project and the requirements in your local jurisdiction, there may be permit fees, demolition costs, and landfill disposal charges to consider. And once your project is complete, be prepared for a possible hike in both your annual property taxes and insurance premiums.

Then, too, it seems Murphy has a special affinity for remodeling projects. Most experts recommend factoring in 10 to 20 percent on top of your budget estimate as a "fudge factor." Particularly with an older home, count on encountering the unexpected. You'll never know exactly what's hiding inside that wall or under that floor until it's way too late to backtrack.

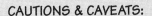
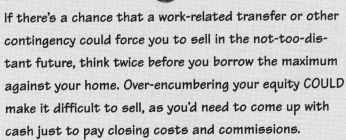

CAUTIONS & CAVEATS:

If there's a chance that a work-related transfer or other contingency could force you to sell in the not-too-distant future, think twice before you borrow the maximum against your home. Over-encumbering your equity COULD make it difficult to sell, as you'd need to come up with cash just to pay closing costs and commissions.

One of the most common budget-busters is the all-too-human tendency to stretch your wish list as you go along. That too-cool hanging lamp is "only" $100 more than you'd expected. And for "just" an extra $500 bucks, you can upgrade to the imported Italian tile that's calling your name.

Resist temptation—or be prepared for a long-term acquaintance with what my friend calls "credit-card purgatory." To help keep yourself on the straight and narrow, draw up an itemized budget before you begin, and refer to it throughout the remodeling to make sure you're staying on track. If you find you're edging significantly over estimate, consider where you might cut back elsewhere—or postpone later portions of the project until your finances catch back up with your fantasies.

Sheer dollars and cents, of course, tell only half the financial-savvy story. When you think "value" as you're budgeting, consider also what you'll get back in terms of quality of life, fewer hassles, and increased durability. The cheapest choice is often NOT the best one.

Finding Financing

Once you've established a budget, how are you going to pay for your new kitchen?

The old-fashioned—and still, in my opinion, best—answer is "with cash." A little financial discipline goes a long way toward making dreams come true. The only drawback, if you're like most of us, is that the "cash" approach means those dreams won't come true tomorrow. It may take a few months—or even a few years—to make it happen.

If you want more instantaneous gratification, there is a wide assortment of financing options available. You can:

Take Out a Second Mortgage: Whether it's a standard second mortgage, a specially designed "home-improvement" loan, or an "equity line of credit," there are many programs designed to lend you money for repair or remodeling costs, secured by the equity in your home. Ask your lender or mortgage broker about any loan-to-equity restrictions; whether the interest rate offered is fixed or variable; the payment amount and term of the loan; and exactly what fees, if any (appraisal, loan application, points, closing costs) you'll be expected to pay. Keep in mind that your lender may set up a "draw" system to disburse the money in stages, as your remodeling progresses. The good news about a loan secured by your personal residence is that the interest MAY be tax-deductible. (Check with your tax advisor to be sure!) But remember, your home will also be at risk for any money you borrow. Make sure you're convinced you can afford the additional monthly payments.

Refinance Your Home: If interest rates have dropped significantly since you purchased or last refinanced your home, it might pay to look into refinancing your existing mortgage for a higher loan balance and using the additional proceeds to pay for your remodeling costs. Fees, points, and closing costs will typically be higher for a refinance than for a home equity loan or

8 WAYS TO KEEP COSTS DOWN

1 Reuse existing fixtures and appliances, or purchase antiques for a quaint and classic look.

2 Haunt salvage and freight-damaged goods shops; scan newspaper advertisements for nearly new appliances or even brand-new building materials.

3 Buy assemble-yourself cabinets, or repaint or reface existing cabinets.

4 Choose stock ceramic tile or vinyl, rather than special-order designs.

equity line of credit, but the interest rate itself is usually a bit lower. If your existing rate is high, it's possible you'll save enough money in the long run to make refinancing worthwhile. Here again, ask about loan-to-equity limits, costs and fees, term choices (usually fifteen or thirty years), total payment (including any impounds that the lender may require), and disbursement schedules.

Look Into Personal Loans. Banks, S&Ls, credit unions, and other lenders offer unsecured or "personal" loans, though the interest rates and other terms are usually much less favorable than loans secured by the equity in your home. Some home-improvement centers also offer a line of credit or in-house credit cards for purchases from their store—usually at fairly stiff rates.

Many credit cards allow you to borrow against your approved line of credit with a check-cashing option. In addition to charging steep interest rates (frequently 19 to 21 percent), credit card issuers may also hit you with a "transaction fee" for the privilege of writing yourself a loan. This can be expensive money. Make sure you know exactly what interest rate and fees will apply.

Ask About Government Loan Programs. There is a wide variety of federal, state, and local home-improvement loan programs available across the country. One of the most popular is the FHA's "Title I" loan. Through the Title I program, you can borrow up to $25,000 for certain basic home repairs and remodeling expenses. You don't have to have equity in your home, and your credit doesn't have to be perfect. The interest rate, however, is going to be higher than for a conventional home-improvement loan, and "luxury" upgrades generally won't qualify. Contact information for the "Title I" loan program is included in the "Sources & Resources" appendix at the end of this book.

Check with your city or county housing authority for information about other home-improvement loan programs in your area. If you live in a designated rehabilitation or historic area, or are a low-income homeowner, there also may be special incentive loan programs available that can help you.

---

8 WAYS TO KEEP COSTS DOWN (continued)

5 Don't make layout changes that will require moving the plumbing or gas lines.

6 Do some or all of the work yourself (painting and papering, for example, make good D-I-Y projects).

7 Consider using less expensive laminates for countertop surfaces; accent with a contrasting edge or ceramic tile back-splash.

8 Bite your tongue every time you find yourself tempted to say the words "while we're at it." Avoid the costly ups-and-extras syndrome!

Locating The Professionals You Need

There is, of course, a wide variety of specialists available to help you with all aspects of your remodeling project—from offering design advice to pounding nails. Just who to call—and how much you should expect to pay—will depend on what help you need, but here are a few basics:

TIP

Legislators just can't seem to keep their hands off the tax codes. For now, at least, capital gains up to $500,000 on the sale of a principal residence may be tax-free at the federal level. And most states have adopted "mirror" legislation applying similar rules at the state tax level. But if you're remodeling a second home—or if you're just plain suspicious that the rules may change—it may pay to keep track of your remodeling receipts to substantiate your increased "tax basis" when you sell. If you're financing the improvements with a loan secured by your home, you'll also want to make a copy of the loan closing statement to keep with your tax papers for the current year—points may be amortizable over the term of the loan, and all or a portion of your closing costs may increase your tax basis.

Architect—If you're planning an extensive kitchen overhaul or major addition, nothing beats the services of a good architect. An architect can provide expert guidance on everything from structural issues to aesthetic nuances. And before you dismiss the idea of working with an architect as "too expensive," remember that good design solutions may actually save you money—and architects' fees ARE often negotiable.

Professional architects are state-licensed, and will have received four to six years of specialized college-level training. They also must meet continuing-education requirements. While not all architects choose to belong, many pay an additional annual fee to become members of the American Institute of Architects; you may recognize the familiar "AIA" letters listed after their names.

An architect may or may not be willing to offer an initial consultation for free—be sure you ask up front. And just how architects charge for their services may also vary. Some will work with you on a flat-fee or price-per-hour basis, doing strictly design work or consulting; others prefer to coordinate the entire job and charge a percentage (usually 5 to 15 percent) of the total cost of the labor and materials used.

As with any professional, word-of-mouth recommendations are often your best source. You can also contact your local AIA chapter (listed in the yellow pages under "Architects"); chapters can direct you to member architects in your area. Ask to take a look at the architect's portfolio. And before you make your final selection, be sure to check references. Ask the architect for a list that you can review.

Before you make your final selection, be sure to check references. Ask the architect for a list of his or her previous kitchen-remodeling clients, and call to inquire how the client thought the experience went. What did they like or not like? Was the result what they expected? How does the final product stack up in the ultimate laboratory of day-to-day-living? Did the job come in on budget—and on time?

If possible, try to VISIT a few of the architect's previous jobs. While some of the choices will have been client-driven, looking at an actual project can give you valuable clues about the architect's design creativity and attention to detail.

Designer—You've no doubt run across several types of "designers." Though they perform very different kinds of services, their titles can be confusingly similar.

A "building designer," like an architect, is trained to draw up plans, estimate costs, and manage/oversee all phases of construction—typically for somewhat less than an architect would charge. While building designers may be familiar with requirements for stresses and loads, they aren't licensed to make such calculations. So if structural work is involved in a project, the services of an architect or engineer may be required and/or your plans may need to go through the "plan check" procedure of your local building department. Unlike architects, whose training includes commercial and industrial design, building designers are trained exclusively to handle residential construction.

Building designers may or may not be state-licensed, depending upon the state in which you live. Many building designers belong to a professional organization known as the American Institute of Building Designers, and add the initials "AIBD" after their

TIPS FROM THE PROS:

"Good design that meets your needs and budget is far more difficult, and takes more time, than a dashed-off solution in which cost is no object. Paying your architect or designer based on a percentage of cost is like handing them a blank check—with no incentive to keep costs under control. It's not only bad business, it can be an invitation to sloppy design."

—Michael Pantano, FCSI (Foodservice Consultants' Society International), commercial kitchen planner and partner in Culinary Advisors, Ellicott City, Maryland

TIPS FROM THE PROS:

"No matter what sort of professional you work with, it's important that women trust their own intuition about what's right for their kitchen. It's so easy to just cave and go along with the 'authority'—whether it's an architect who insists on using recessed lighting, or a plumber who thinks you need multiple sinks. Sure, you should listen and ask questions. But don't be afraid to stand up for what you really think will work best. The times I felt railroaded into decisions, I've regretted them later. And I knew in my heart all the time they weren't right."

—Cindi Dixon, illustrator and photographer

names. Some elect to pursue further education and testing to qualify for the "certified professional building designer (CPBD)" credential.

Some building designers allow you to schedule a one-time consultation to simply pick their brains about design ideas, product choices, and perhaps money-saving suggestions. Others will want to coordinate the entire job—and charge accordingly.

Another type of design professional is the "certified kitchen designer," or CKD. A CKD has passed a series of tests administered by the National Kitchen & Bath Association (a manufacturers' trade organization), and must have at least seven years of experience and/or education in the kitchen design industry. CKDs may work independently, but more frequently you'll find them affiliated with a kitchen business or showroom, where they often work on commission. The NKBA publishes a free directory of CKDs—call (908) 852-0033 for information. On occasion, uncertified sales staff in a kitchen design company or product showroom may also be somewhat casually referred to as "designers" or "kitchen designers."

Many specialized kitchen businesses offer a range of "design/build" services in connection with their storefront or showroom. These companies can not only help you design your kitchen, but have their own licensed contractors on-staff to do the actual work, or have formed special affiliations with local contractors. They'll quote you a firm price and offer the convenience of "one-stop shopping," with a chance to preview materials in a showroom-type setting. Remember, however, that the salesperson who works with you is typically on commission.

If you're seeking advice on aesthetic finishing touches, you may want to consider hiring an *interior designer or interior decorator*. Both interior designers and interior decorators can help with decorating, paint, appliances, furnishings, lighting, and fabric choices, and will have sample books or swatches available to make such choices easier. Many will also be able to suggest contractors, help coordinate the job, or offer guidance for do-it-yourselfers. While virtually anyone can call him- or herself a "decorator," interior designers generally hold some more formal type of certification. Members of the American Society of Interior Designers (ASID), for example, must meet educational and/or work experience criteria and pass a two-day accreditation exam; some ASID members are also architects. ASID can connect you with members in your area. Call (800) 775-2743 or visit their Web site at www.asid.org or www.interiors.org (referrals).

Draftsman—If you already know exactly what you want in your kitchen and just need someone to draw up a set of plans—perhaps to submit for a building permit, or to allow you to solicit contractor bids—you may simply prefer to hire a draftsman. He or she may have studied technical rendering at a trade school, or just learned through on-the-job experience working for an engineer or contractor. While a good draftsman can draw up a set of plans, unlike an architect he or she is not trained to calculate stresses and loads. Some draftsmen have extensive experience in the building industry and may be able to give you basic guidance on costs and materials. But that's really not their forte.

A local contractor may be able to recommend a good draftsman (though many contractors draw their own plans). Or check the Yellow Pages under "Drafting Services."

Other Sources of Information: Home-improvement stores often offer free design help and remodeling advice, and many now have computerized programs to help you visualize what your kitchen will look like when the remodeling is complete. In addition to the cabi-

TIP

Don't let wishful "on-paper" thinking blind you to the realities of comfortable clearances. Before you decide to add an island, stretch a counter, or shoe-horn in a pantry, evaluate how the proposed change will affect your space and movements by marking its outline on the floor with masking tape. Can you still open the refrigerator door? Will you have to sidle sideways to reach the pantry? Er, back to the drawing board!

nets, fixtures, and appliances on display, these stores generally can special-order a wide range of other products.

The "do-it-yourself" crowd will also find a myriad of design tools on the market today. Computer-aided design (CAD) programs for use on a home computer are available at just about any office supply or software dealer. Less high-tech but also visually helpful are "magnetic" vinyl design kits, which contain cut-out pieces drawn to represent standard cabinet widths and appliances that can be easily arranged and rearranged on a background grid. Ask at your local home-improvement center, or check the ads in remodeling magazines.

And don't discount the value of the good, old-fashioned pencil and graph paper. Once you've got a scale drawing of your current layout, an overlay of tracing paper can help you decide how you might like to move things around.

Coping With Contractors—And Contracts!

If you'd prefer not to be involved in coordinating the day-to-day construction work— and particularly if you're planning a complex, expensive remodeling project—an architect or other design professional can shoulder the burden of hiring and overseeing the work of contractors and subcontractors for you. For smaller jobs, tighter budgets, and simply folks who prefer a more "hands-on" management approach, however, you'll probably find yourself dealing with one or more contractors.

Contractors come in several flavors. Many general contractors are used to handling all types of construction (from new buildings to retrofits, commercial or residential); but some specialize strictly in remodels. Some contractors are licensed only as "subcontractors," and perform only portions of the job, such as plumbing or electrical work.

CAUTIONS & CAVEATS:

Most states now require contractors to be licensed—but a few do not. If your state has a licensing law, however, you may not be able to recover for defective work if you hire an unlicensed contractor! Check with your state's contractors licensing agency or consumer-protection officials to find out more about licensing requirements.

Whatever type of contractor you wind up hiring, there's no substitute for experience—preferably somebody else's! Ask friends, relatives, neighbors and co-workers for recommendations. Once you've found a likely prospect, ask the contractor for references and CALL them. Were they happy with the work? The price? The time within which the job was completed? The cleanup?

Make sure any contractor you're considering is licensed and that his license is still in good standing by calling your state contractors' license board. Ask whether a history of action against the contractor is available: Has his license ever been suspended or revoked? Have there been any court judgments against him, paid or not? Has he posted a license bond—and when does it expire?

Ditto on double-checking insurance coverage: Make sure your contractor carries not only workers' compensation insurance, but also personal liability and property damage coverage, and verify what he tells you with his insurance carrier or agent.

One way to gauge a contractor's creditworthiness is to ask for the names of suppliers from whom he regularly buys materials, and inquire whether supply bills are generally paid on time (some businesses may require a signed letter of permission from the contractor before they will disclose such information to you). A phone call to the Better Business Bureau and your local consumer protection agency may be able to tell you if there have been recent complaints by unhappy clients. You can also sometimes learn a lot simply from what your local building inspector is willing to say—or not say—if you drop in and mention the contractor's name.

Appearance isn't everything, but sometimes it can give you valuable clues about both a contractor's work ethic and whether he's operating on a shoestring. Are his tools neatly organized, or jumbled in a heap? Is his truck a junkyard gem sporting three bald tires and a spare? Does he arrive an hour late for your appointment looking as though he just rolled out of bed? Consider any of those at least a serious caution flag.

TIPS FROM THE PROS:

"You and your contractor should discuss in detail exactly what work is going to be performed, what materials are to be used, who will purchase the materials, all costs, and the estimated time involved. Everything should be clearly stated in writing. As we all know, 'money changes everything.' Therefore your initial deposit to the contractor should be as small as possible and final payment should be contingent upon the work being completed on time and to your satisfaction."

—Marie Cappuccio, attorney

TIPS FROM THE PROS

"The best contracts provide for a method of dispute resolution—your contractor may be able to tell you if there is a local organization that can help resolve problems. The contract may also state that any future disputes will be resolved through arbitration, mediation, or some combination of the two. There are many private agencies such as the American Arbitration Association that can inexpensively address construction disputes. Just remember that if your contract provides for MANDATORY arbitration, you will not be able to disregard that agreement later and pursue a claim in court; you will have committed to arbitrate instead."

—Marie Cappuccio, attorney

Make sure you're comfortable with your contractor on a personal level, too. After all, you will probably be spending a great deal of time together. If you'll be the one directly supervising the job, ask straight out how they feel about working for a woman. Pay attention to body language as well as their words. Do they make eye contact? Are they listening to what you want, or do they talk over you? Do they inspire confidence and a sense of rapport? Or do you find them standoffish or perhaps even arrogant?

Putting It in Writing

The usual rule of thumb is to get three bids in writing before choosing a contractor. But make sure you're comparing apples with apples when you get to the bottom line. Is each contractor offering to perform the same scope of work and the same quality of materials?

Think twice or even three times before snapping up the lowest bid, particularly if it's *significantly* lower than the other two. There's most likely a reason—and you probably won't like it. Be cautious, also, about accepting any bid on a time-and-materials (or "T&M") basis. The contractor may say that it's hard to know what conditions he may encounter, and may emphasize that you'll be paying only for the actual work received. The problem, of course, is that he has no incentive to conserve either time OR materials, since you'll be paying for both. If at all possible, push for a fixed dollar amount instead.

Once you decide which bid to accept, the contractor will either ask you to sign the bid itself, or present you with a separate contract form that incorporates the bid terms. Either way, it becomes a binding contract when both of you have signed, so be sure you read it CAREFULLY and understand all terms before signing.

The contract should describe the work that is to be completed, list appliances and other materials (with model, brand, size, color) to be provided, identify the total price and payment schedule, and give a fixed or estimated completion date. The contractor's name, address, and phone number are often stamped right on the form; make sure the contractor's license number is also included. One phrase that should raise at least a red flag if not flashing lights and sirens: "or equal"—a term that means the contractor can substitute other materials of comparable quality. If a particular brand is important to you, be sure that's specified.

If you have any questions or qualms about what's in the contract, don't hesitate to ask for a day or two to run it by a lawyer—if possible, one who regularly handles real estate law—before signing. No reputable contractor will try to rush you into a decision.

Be sure you negotiate a payment schedule you're comfortable with—and that what you have agreed upon is fully reflected in your contract. If it's a large job, expect to pay a percentage up front (in some states, there's a statutory cap on what contractors can demand in advance). You may be expected to make "progress payments" as the work reaches certain milestones, with a final payment due "upon completion." But aside from the down payment, don't let your contractor pressure you to pre-pay for work not yet completed because he "needs to buy materials." Owing your contractor money is your best (and sometimes, your only) leverage to make sure the job is done and done to your satisfaction. It's a good idea—and common practice—to write a holdback or "retention" of at least 10 percent of the contract price right into the contract, payable only when all punch list items are completed.

Ask your contractor to help you try to anticipate possible construction delays and obstacles ahead of time. Talk about where he can store materials on-site before they're installed (you don't want your brand-new cabinets sitting out in the rain). Find out how your contractor plans to handle trash removal—are they hiring a Dumpster? What will that cost—and who gets to pay for it? If you suspect there may be lead-based paint,

TIP:

If you plan to finance the cost of your home-improvement project but your loan hasn't gone through yet, you may want to hold off signing any agreement with your contractor until your loan is formally approved. At the very least, make sure your contract specifies that it is contingent upon obtaining acceptable financing and may be subject to certain additional requirements (such as a progress payment schedule) imposed by the lender.

Problems

TIP:

Don't give the go-ahead for any changes without knowing how much extra it will cost and putting the "change order" details in writing. A few casual remarks such as "Sure," "Fine," or "Sounds good to me," as you're walking around the job site with your contractor can cost you big bucks. Remember, too, that some changes should actually SAVE you money. If you decide to go with a smaller window than originally planned, for example, the contractor may owe you a credit.

Is your sink installed crooked, tile the wrong color, one cabinet missing—and the contractor's dunning you for sums you paid months ago? If you've got a problem with workmanship or a dispute over payment, don't despair:

- ✎ Take it up with your contractor first, face-to-face—and preferably right on the job site, where you can point to and he can inspect the problem. Be clear about what's wrong and talk about ways to make it right.

- ✎ If you're still not able to resolve the dispute, contact your state's contractors license board and ask about the procedure for filing a complaint. Also ask if they offer arbitration programs or other dispute-resolution assistance.

- ✎ Read your contract. Have you both agreed to binding arbitration? If so, under what agency or rules? Even if your contract doesn't require mandatory arbitration, you may be able to convince your contractor to arbitrate the dispute voluntarily, or to try to informally work out your differences through mediation. Arbitration programs may be offered by your state's contractors license board (see bullet point above). Arbitration is also available through the American Arbitration Association and other professional dispute-resolution groups. Some attorneys also provide mediation services. Check your Yellow Pages under "arbitrators" and check the attorney listings under "arbitration" and "mediation."

- ✎ If the dollar amount in dispute is not large, consider taking the matter to small-claims court. Your local court clerk can usually provide you with the necessary forms and instructions about how to prepare and file them.

✎ For larger disputes, talk with an attorney—preferably a real estate attorney. (Even where the up-front dispute is simply one of payment or nonpayment, a business or debtor/creditor attorney may not be your best bet. Underlying issues in construction cases often involve construction techniques, liens, and building materials, so it's usually a good idea to find a lawyer with experience handling construction disputes.) Ask friends and relatives for a referral, or contact your local bar association.

How can you spot a home improvement rip-off coming?

Often, it's hard to tell. Really great scam artists can be thoroughly charming. But here is a list of tip-offs to common cons:

✎ Beware of any firm that insists on being paid only in cash.

✎ Beware door-to-door solicitors, high-pressure sales tactics, special pricing for agreeing to participate in a "demonstration" project, or a discount if you refer other clients.

✎ Be suspicious of materials "left over" from a previous job.

✎ Beware "no-problem financing" that a contractor claims he can obtain through a "friend."

✎ Always get a second opinion before authorizing any "urgent" repair work a contractor claims he's suddenly discovered is necessary.

✎ NEVER sign papers with blanks that are not filled in, or which contain any term you don't understand.

Source: The Bureau of Consumer Protection and General Services Administration. For the full text of a variety of helpful consumer education publications available on-line, go to: <www.ftc.gov/bcp/menu-home.htm> and <www.pueblo.gsa.gov/housing.htm>

TIPS FROM THE PROS:

"How to find a good contractor? Choose somebody who loves what he's doing and is obviously excited about his work. And if you happen to be a writer, it never hurts to promise to write him up in an article!"

—Rose Levy Beranbaum, author of seven books including *The Cake Bible* (named Cookbook of the Year by the Int'l Assoc. of Culinary Professionals/Seagram) and *The Pie and Pastry Bible*

asbestos or other hazardous materials present in your home, have it inspected BEFORE soliciting bids to avoid last-minute surprises.

No matter how thoroughly you try to anticipate, however, there likely will be a few problems that crop up as the remodeling work progresses. Perhaps a plumbing line concealed in the wall needs repair, or the building inspector requires you to add a new vent. That appliance that looked as though it would fit perfectly on paper turns out to need more clearance than you expected. In older homes, it's possible that remodeling may uncover asbestos or other hazardous materials. Or in a worst-case scenario, you might run into *all* of those problems.

A good contractor will be a good problem-solver, and should be able to help you come up with a solution for most any obstacle. But solutions are not always cheap and your contractor shouldn't be expected to do extra work for free. If additional work becomes necessary (or you just decide to gild the lily and throw in a few extras as you go along!), make sure either you or your contractor writes up a "change order" each time, specifying exactly what additional materials or services you've agreed to and what they will cost. Both you and your contractor should sign each change order and you each should have a copy to keep.

As the job draws to a close, you'll usually have a "punch list" of items for the contractor to fix or finish. Perhaps there's a short strip of molding missing, a broken tile that needs to be replaced, or a nail pop to fix. By now you may be feeling as though your contractor is

Keep A Job File:

Before your remodeling project begins, start a "job file" where you can keep important papers. Here's a partial list of what you might want to include in your file:

✓ Contract(s).

✓ Change orders and any other notes or correspondence with your contractor.

✓ Copies of plans or specifications (unroll and fold blueprints).

CAUTIONS & CAVEATS:

Subcontractors and material suppliers also have lien rights. If your contractor has an electrician, plumber, cabinetmaker and other subcontractors working under him, and/or if materials are delivered from a lumber store or other supply house, ask for a signed full or partial lien release from each subcontractor and material provider as proof that they've been paid, before you hand over each major disbursement and the final contract balance.

practically a member of the family. You've probably shared your home with him for weeks! Still, don't write that final check until every item on your punch list has been checked off.

Permits & Other Practical Details

Will you need to obtain a building permit before beginning your remodeling? That all depends, of course, on your local ordinances and what work you plan to do. You'll definitely need a permit if you plan any structural changes—moving walls or adding windows, for example. You'll probably also need one for any serious plumbing or electrical work.

To find out exactly what permits will be required (and what they will cost), ask your local planning or building department. You will probably be required to submit a set of plans with your permit application. If window changes are part of your remodeling wish list, some jurisdictions may also require you to submit detailed thermal efficiency data, sometimes known as "energy calcs" or "heat calcs."

If you hire a general contractor, make sure your contract specifies that the contractor will obtain all necessary building permits (and expect that you will ultimately pay any associated permit fees). If you're acting as your own general contractor, it will be up to you to obtain the necessary permits.

Remember that a permit isn't just a fee; a building inspector will visit and take a look at work in progress to make sure it's being done to code. I always like to be present whenever an inspection is scheduled, both to answer any questions that may come up and to hear firsthand what items the inspector may want changed. If you've hired a general contractor, however, it's only courteous to let him or her deal directly with the inspector. Remember, your contractor's reputation is at stake.

Keep A Job File: (continued)

✓ Building permit(s) (these usually stay on the job site during the work, but should go in your file when signed off).

✓ Receipts for materials and bills, marked when paid.

✓ A list of subcontractors and material suppliers, their pre-lien notices (if any), and lien releases.

✓ A log of job progress, including start date, deliveries, weather or other delays.

✓ "Before," "during," and "after" photos.

Insurance: *Are You Covered?*

Check with your insurance agent before you begin your remodeling project to make sure your coverage is adequate. Are materials that have been delivered but not yet installed covered under your policy? Who's responsible if your contractor's expensive tools get stolen? What about on-the-job injuries to day laborers you hire yourself, or employees of subcontractors who fail to carry workers' compensation insurance?

You'll also need to update your policy to reflect any increased value of your home after remodeling. And be sure to ask about premium discounts if you've upgraded your electrical system, installed sprinklers, or added smoke detectors.

One final insurance caution: If you're hiring a contractor to do some or all of the work, ask whether he carries workers' compensation, personal liability, and property damage coverage. Then call his carrier or agent to verify that the policy is in force.

Doing It Yourself

Working on your own home can be a great way to learn skills you've always wanted to master. You can take your time and learn as you go. And if you do make a mistake—well, that's part of how we learn, too!

When you come right down to it, there are probably few parts of a kitchen remodeling that you CAN'T learn to do, given sufficient time, motivation, and perhaps a strong helper or two. The real question is how much you WANT to tackle. Remember that on-the-job training can be time-consuming; doing it yourself may mean your kitchen project takes considerably longer than it would if you simply hire a pro. You may not just have to learn new skills, but also buy new tools (though for some of us, that's a plus!) Mistakes can also be expensive. One mismeasured cabinet or "oops" with a saw could cost you more than you've "saved" by doing it yourself.

On the other hand, even if you're not angling for "Handywoman of the Year," there are some jobs that give a great return for a relatively small investment of time and low-tech labor. Painting is one. And myself, I've always loved ceramic tile work.

Bottom line: If you WANT to learn to a remodeling skill, your own kitchen project can be a great learning laboratory. Buy a few how-to books; watch project-specific videos; ask a knowledgeable friend to coach you through it the first time. But if you'd really be happier *not* spending your weekends becoming intimately acquainted with the aisles of the local home-improvement store, don't apologize. Let your checkbook do the heavy lifting.

Survival Skills: Life During The Remodeling

Sawdust. Plaster dust. House dust. And just plain tracked-in dirt. Count on the fact that your kitchen will be Ground Zero of a disaster area for days, weeks, possibly even months.

To minimize (or at least contain) the inevitable fallout, tape plastic sheeting over doorways while demolition is going on, and make sure adjacent wood floors, carpeting, and furniture in nearby rooms and traffic ways are protected. You may also want to cover outside decks with sheets of plywood to protect the surface if they'll be tromped over constantly or used to store construction materials.

Before construction gets under way, remove and store anything in your kitchen that you don't want to get dirty or broken—pots, pans, dishes, utensils, appliances.

If you know you're going to be kitchenless for any period of time, set up a temporary "camp" kitchen in another room of the house with a microwave, coffeemaker, trash can, and perhaps a mini-fridge. You may not want to host any lavish banquets or invite your mother-in-law to dinner, but you can at least enjoy a cup of coffee in the morning and reheat frozen dinners in a pinch.

TIP:

Be REALISTIC about how long your remodeling project is going to take. Keep a master-scheduling calendar to help keep track of when contractors, subcontractors, inspectors, and material deliveries should be arriving. Count on unforeseen delays—so avoid schedules that could conflict with weddings, holidays or other family events if the timing runs over. The sanity you save may be your own.

Little Things That Make A Difference

Tired of the way your current kitchen looks, but suffering a bad case of the budget blues? Not to worry. Here's a range of checkbook-friendly changes that can add sizzle to your kitchen—without landing your finances in hot water.

Cabinet Pulls

They've been called "jewelry for your cabinets" and it's easy to see why. Exotic cabinet pulls run the gamut from polished brass to painted porcelain, from jewel-toned glass to sparkling chrome. If you're tired of plain-Jane plastic handles or simple wooden knobs, you're just a screwdriver-twist away from a whole new look!

Most cabinet *knobs* will be interchangeable. But if you're purchasing replacement pulls or handles, be wary about screw spacing. Hole pairs may be spaced 2 3/4, 3,

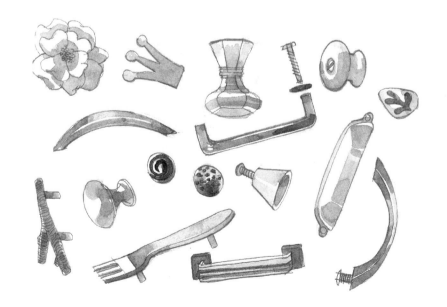

3 1/2 inches or even farther apart. And some of the new "Euro" styles now use metric spacing.

Sure, in most cases you can always drill a brand new hole to accommodate a different-size pull. But unless you're planning to paint (or repaint) your cabinets, it may be difficult or impossible to patch the old hole without leaving an unsightly repair. It's easiest to simply try to match your existing hole pattern. Measure the distance between the existing holes center-to-center to determine the correct screw spacing; or better yet, take one of the old handles with you when you purchase replacements.

Your local hardware store or home-improvement center will offer a wide range of hardware options, from bright and inexpensive plastic to downright pricey (but worth every penny) solid brass. If your taste runs to antiques, try haunting estate sales for the genuine article or check renovators' catalogs for reproduction, vintage-style hardware. And if you're really after a "different" look, check out the custom-crafted hardware advertised in decorating and remodeling magazines. But remember that specialty items may not be cheap; some deluxe decorator versions can run $100 per pull—or (choke) even more!

TIP:

Want to try sculpting your own custom cabinet knobs? Check your local crafts store for make-it-and-bake-it crafts clay. Shape over a wooden pull, bake as directed, then splash on colorful acrylic paint for your own fabulously functional works of art.

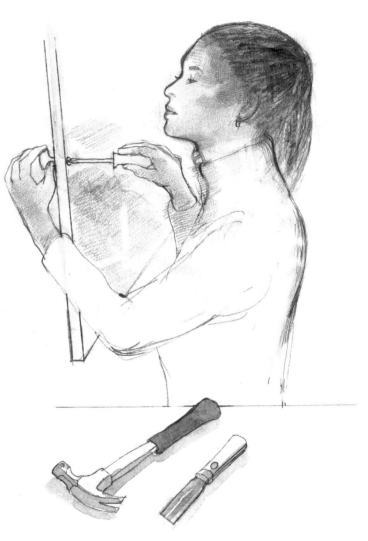

Paint

For sheer simplicity—and cost-consciousness—there's nothing quite like the power of paint. For less than $100, you can brighten and lighten, touch up and tweak, or totally transform the look of your kitchen.

And while women have long known about the power of paint, the paint companies, it seems, have now discovered womanpower as well. Stop in at virtually any home-improvement store these days, and you'll find designer names on paint charts and helpful "how-to" brochures for faux-paint finishes.

When it comes to choosing paint, the most important thing isn't the designer label, but what's *inside* the can. Cheaper paints often have high clay content—an inexpensive "filler" that doesn't provide either the coverage or body of costlier pigments. Particularly when you're changing wall colors, a better grade of paint can often do the same job in just one coat that a cheaper brand may take two—or more—to accomplish. That "expensive" can, in other words, may ultimately save you time and money. For dependable performance, stick with a tried-and-true name brand, or ask your paint store to recommend a top-quality paint.

What about using primer? Primers are recommended on bare wood, as a first coat on new drywall, or if you've got oil-based paint and want to switch to latex. They'll also help improve coverage if you're painting dark walls a lighter shade. And you may also

Tip:

• Most paint and home-improvement stores can now match the color of just about anything. Bring in a pillow, a scrap of wallpaper, or even your favorite sweater, and their computer will scan the color and spit out the paint formula for an exact, look-alike shade. Especially with such custom-mixed colors, however, be sure you protect the coded mixing label that your paint store affixes to the can. Before you even open the can (and run the risk of dripping paint on that magic formula), cover the label with clear plastic tape—that's crucial information if you ever need to match the color at a later date.

• Ask your paint or hardware store to tint your primer paint a shade or two lighter than your final top coat will be. The similar shade will help you achieve good coverage, while allowing you to easily spot any places you miss with the final coat.

Latex or oil?

One of the most basic paint hurdles you'll need to cross is whether to choose latex or oil-based paint. Most of today's "oil" paints are actually alkyd—a special blend of oil and synthetic resin formulated to minimize the off-gassing of volatile organic compounds or "VOCs."

The primary advantage of latex paint—and it's a big one—is easy water cleanup. Just rinse brushes and rollers in water, and they're ready for your next painting party. Latex paint is also faster-drying than oil, and tends to be a little less smelly in the process. Oil paints, by contrast, tend be more expensive; and because they require a chemical solvent for cleanup, will require a bit more effort on the back end of the job. But they'll repay that extra investment with exceptional body and shine, and generally will provide a more durable interior finish.

One important consideration before you make that final latex-vs.-oil decision: as a rule of thumb, it's best to stick with whatever type of paint is already on your walls. Can't stand latex? You can probably paint over it with oil-based paint if you really want (try a small, out-of-the-way section first, just to be certain!) But if you've got oil-based paint on your walls and want to switch to latex instead, it's not quite so easy. You'll have to use a special primer first to ensure that the latex paint will stick. Ask about an appropriate primer at your paint store.

Not quite sure what kind of paint is presently on your walls? At least one manufacturer now makes a swab-type test kit that'll give you a quick, definite answer. A simple though less definitive alternative: Scrape the edge of a real silver coin (not today's copper-sandwich type) across the painted surface. Silver leaves a pencil-like line on oil-based paint, but will make only a faint mark on rubbery latex.

Note:

Research now points to latex as the superior choice for **exterior** applications. The reasons: Latex paints are more flexible, and thus can expand or contract with variations in temperature without checking or cracking as much as the less-resilient oil paints. And because latex is more porous than oil-based paints, water vapor is less apt to build up behind the paint layer and cause peeling or blisters.

want to consider spot-treating grease or water stains with a primer-sealer before painting, to prevent these stains from bleeding through your final coat.

Traditionally, kitchens were painted with a gloss or semi-gloss finish for high clean-ability. Today's paint lines now include eggshell and satin finishes if you prefer a less shiny but still washable alternative. And several manufacturers now offer specially formulated, scrubbable flat paints. Whatever sheen you apply to your walls, semi-gloss or gloss is still the top choice for molding, doors, woodwork, and other "high-impact" areas. When selecting a finish, however, remember that the higher the shine, the more you'll notice any flaws in the painted surface.

Picked your paint, selected your shade, finalized the finish? Whatever the paint you've chosen, the key to a great-looking end result is painstaking preparation. Because grease tends to be a problem on kitchen walls, make sure you clean wall surfaces thoroughly before you begin. Use a trisodium phosphate (TSP) solution to cut grease and slightly etch the surface to help ensure good adhesion. Be sure to rinse walls thoroughly with clear water, and allow to dry completely before beginning (a full day, if possible). And speaking of dry: Check the weather before you begin. It's best not to schedule a paint job during wet or exceptionally humid weather.

If you're starting with an extra-shiny surface, sand with fine-grit sandpaper and consider adding a bonding agent (available at paint stores) to your paint to improve adhe-

TIP: Weather Matters!
Before you start that painting project, it's a good idea to double-check your local weather forecast. Some manufacturers specify a recommended temperature range for applying their paints (50 to 90 degrees for latex paint, for example). And paint takes longer to dry during wet weather or periods of high humidity.

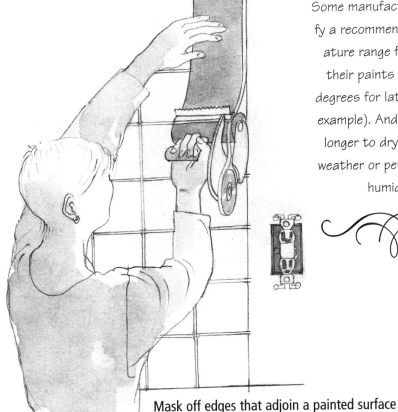

Mask off edges that adjoin a painted surface

Tools Of The Trade

You'll find a wide range of both quality and prices when it comes to painting tools. My best advice: Don't scrimp! Cheap rollers will break under pressure or allow the roller cover to "walk"; bottom-of-the-line brushes have an annoying tendency to shed their bristles and simply don't hold much paint; "bargain" roller covers can leave fuzz on the walls. Good-quality tools will pay for themselves again and again in ease of use and lack of hassle. Here are some of the tools you'll need:

- 9-inch roller
- Roller handle extension
- Roller cover
- Paint opener (key)
- Stir stick
- Roller tray or bucket grate
- Angled 2-inch brush
- Small trim brush for window mullions and other fine work
- Metal-edged paint shield

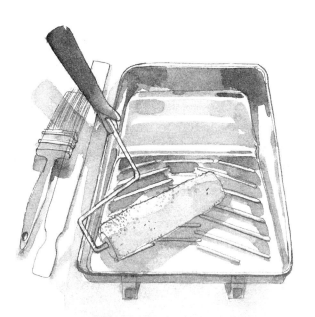

sion. Spackle any cracks or nail holes, and sand any area where the existing paint is uneven or flaking. (CAUTION: See lead paint hazard cautions on page 57.)

Though some folks say it's possible to paint right over wallpaper, my advice is DON'T. Rent or buy a steamer, strip the walls, clean them thoroughly to remove any remaining paste, and start fresh.

Once the walls have been prepped, give yourself as much working space as possible. Clear everything off your counters (you don't want paint flecks on your favorite canisters) and relocate trash cans, rolling carts, plants, and so on to another room of the house. Protect woodwork and counter backsplashes by masking off edges that adjoin a painted surface, and cover appliances and flooring with dropcloths.

You'll also need to remove switchplate and outlet covers on the walls you'll be painting. It's a good idea to collect the covers and screws in a small box or other container (I use a coffee can) as you go, so you won't break or lose them. Note: If you have children or pets who might be tempted by accessible wires or if you're simply a bit skittish about electricity yourself, turn off the power to your kitchen circuits (there may be more than one) at your fuse box or electrical panel before removing switch and outlet covers. And since your electricity may be off for a while, don't forget that you may need to plug your refrigerator into another circuit to keep food cold.

Ready to roll?

Chances are, your paint or hardware store will put your paint container on a "shaking machine" to mix it thoroughly before you bring it home. If you're using paint that's been sitting in your garage for any length of time, however, give the can a good stirring before you begin to use it.

Painting Cabinets:

Yes, you can paint over most kitchen cabinets—even those with "wood-look" or laminate finishes (test in an inconspicuous spot first, to make sure). Clean cabinets well with a TSP solution to remove grease; rinse and allow to dry. Then remove cabinet doors, and sand face frames and doors with a fine-grit sandpaper to roughen the surface and help the paint stick. Apply a primer coat, then follow with one or two coats of gloss or semigloss. Because cabinets take such constant wear and tear, use an alkyd ("oil-based") primer and paint.

Tip:

How much paint to buy?? The honest if not exactly helpful answer is, "It depends." The amount of paint you'll need will vary depending on how well a particular brand covers, what color you're aiming for (and painting over), and the type of surface (porous; nonporous) you'll be applying it to. For help in estimating, bring a scale drawing of your kitchen's dimensions with you to the paint store, and ask them to help you calculate the number of gallons of each type paint (flat, semi-gloss, primer, etc.) you'll need. "Paint calculators" are also available on-line at do-it-yourself Web sites and paint company home pages.

Assemble your roller by sliding a roller cover over the metal frame (most roller covers are well-labeled; choose a thin nap for smooth surfaces, and a thicker nap for textured walls). Since you'll be painting the ceiling first, also screw the extension handle into the base of the roller to give you more reach.

Pour paint into a roller tray, or partially fill a 5-gallon bucket and slip a roller grate over the edge. Dip your roller into the paint, and squeeze out the excess against the tray ridges or roller grate. You want the roller cover to be thoroughly wet but not drippy.

Begin in one corner of the ceiling and roll a pattern about three feet square at a time before moving on to the next section. Make sure you overlap strokes slightly to eliminate "lines"; if necessary, go back over the area in a different direction while the paint is still wet to ensure a random look. You'll quickly figure out what pattern works best for you and gives a uniform-looking coverage.

Once the ceiling is done, start on the walls. Don't try to get too close to electrical outlets, door molding, or baseboards; you'll be able to get those areas more easily with a brush when you go back for what's called "cutting in."

A small pause here to mention a bit of painting controversy: some folks prefer to do their cutting in first, before they roll the ceiling and walls. I've always found it's easier to see exactly what needs to be cut in if I do things the other way around. (And, of course, by doing the roller work first, you get that splash of instant color gratification!)

Last but not least, tackle the doors, baseboard, and trim. Use a metal-edged paint shield to help you keep paint away from floor tile and other adjacent surfaces.

You'll want to remove any masking tape fairly quickly to keep it from leaving a sticky adhesive residue. Be sure to allow paint to dry thoroughly, however, before replacing electrical covers or stirring up any dust.

cleanup & storage

✎ If you're just taking a break for lunch, stow paint-brushes and rollers inside a plastic food-storage bag temporarily so they don't dry out while you're gone. You can even wrap an entire roller tray with a large plastic trash bag to save cleanup during short absences. (Just don't forget what's UNDER that lumpy black plastic and step on it when you return!)

✎ Always follow manufacturer's instructions for paint cleanup. And don't put that chore off. If you hope to salvage your tools for future painting jobs, take care of them as soon as possible.

✎ Make sure paint cans seal tightly by cleaning away excess paint on the lip before replacing the lid.

✎ For long-term storage, keep leftover paint in its original can so you'll remember the exact brand and type. Use a felt-tipped permanent marker to label the lid ("Kitchen 12/99," for example) for easy touch-up reference. Just make sure you don't write over that crucial mixing code.

Lead Paint Cautions:

Hold that sandpaper! Could your home have lead-based paint?

Sanding, scraping, and even heating lead-based paint can pose a serious health threat, particularly to children and pregnant women. If your home was built before 1978, there is a strong possibility that some or all of the older coats of paint on your walls and woodwork contain lead. Contact the National Lead Clearinghouse (NLC) at 1-800-424-LEAD for information about special precautions that should be taken in order to work safely with lead paint.

A number of do-it-yourself test kits claim to be able to detect lead in paint and other materials. For greatest accuracy, choose a test that offers mail-in laboratory results. You may also want to consider calling in an expert to test your home for lead. The NLC can provide you with a list of individuals and organizations that offer lead-based paint inspections, risks assessments, and hazard-control services. Call 1-888-LEADLIST for more information.

Flourishes & Faux Finishes

There are probably as many variations on the "faux-finish" theme as there are faux-finish fanciers, but here's a basic introduction to several popular techniques. Always practice on a test patch before beginning. Some folks recommend experimenting on a sheet of cardboard or scrap of drywall; for others, the tried-and-true favorite is the inside of a little-used closet.

Sponging:

One of the easiest "faux" techniques to master, sponging gives a mottled or dappled appearance that's great for adding texture and interest to Plain Jane spaces. Begin by painting walls a solid base color in an eggshell or satin finish. Let dry. Dip a damp sea sponge in a contrasting color, and dab gently in a random pattern. (Tear off small sponge pieces for corners and out-of-the-way spots.) Add a second sponged-on color if you wish, for additional interest. Dilute the top (sponge) coats with water or with the paint manufacturer's own "glazing liquid" for a more subtle, translucent effect.

Ragging:

Ragging also begins with a solid base color in a slightly reflecting (eggshell or satin) finish. Thinned paint in a contrasting color is then "ragged on" using a cheesecloth or old cotton T-shirt in a gentle blotting motion, or applied with a standard paint roller and then "ragged off." For a bolder variation, try using a paper or plastic bag instead of the soft rag. "Ragging on" gives a dramatic and less polished flavor; "ragging off" lends a softer, more subtle result.

Color Washing:

This technique uses very dilute ("wash") topcoats, applied or blended with a brush for a rustic effect. Brush or rag on a first wash over dry base paint. Let this coat dry before brushing on a second wash in a contrasting color. Or sponge on the second wash while the first wash is still wet, and blend with a wide brush.

Stenciling:

Create borders, decorative accents, or even faux "wallpaper" using stencil cutouts. Purchase commercial kits at a crafts store, or make your own by tracing a design onto stiff acetate and cutting with a razor knife. Imaginative stencil suggestions from painting pros include stars, paw prints, leafy borders, and even words (sure, there's always "home sweet home," but how about a running legend over your backsplash repeating your favorite verse?) Begin with a level pencil line as a guide, and use masking tape or spray adhesive to keep the stencil from slipping as you work. You'll probably want to experiment with colors on a large sheet of paper first; tape the paper up to your wall to get an idea of how it will look. Use a separate stencil for each color. Dab paint on gently with a stencil brush or sponge. (For best results, keep your brush or sponge relatively dry.)

working with color

Don't be afraid of color! Gone are the days when the only acceptable choices for interior walls were tepid taupes, boring beiges, and lukewarm whites.

Color shifts can help to separate areas within your home, while a common color theme can unify adjoining rooms. Let color help you emphasize a focal point by painting one wall a different shade, for example. Or bring attention to crown molding or the back of a built-in bookcase with a snappy contrasting shade. (Remember, however, that high contrast and intense colors will tend to make a room seem smaller.) Color can also help you create a little fool-the-eye magic in awkward spaces: "Lower" a too-high ceiling by painting it several shades darker than the surrounding walls, or "raise" it by choosing a color that's paler.

Let color help you set the mood you're after—reds and other deep jewel tones can lend drama and excitement, while pale pastels are more soothing. Your climate may also be a factor you'll want to consider; to add warmth, think peach and terra cotta. For a cool, airy freshness, you might opt instead for shades of blue or green. To brighten a dark or north-facing room, try a sunny yellow.

It's tough, of course, to figure out what your kitchen will actually look like simply by staring at those tiny color chips. A few manufacturers have taken pity on us and now offer slightly larger examples. But the only real way to tell how a color will look on your walls is to try it. Buy the smallest quantity your paint or hardware store sells, and paint a sample patch. It's easy enough to paint over if you don't like it. (If you're really chicken, you can always try it out on a large piece of cardboard first.)

Give yourself time to really study the effect. A color will look different in early morning and at dusk, in the bright sunlight streaming through a window and by candlelight.

Wallpaper & Borders

You either love it or you hate it. My own feelings about the matter were sealed when I spent days (it felt like weeks) stripping multiple layers from just one room of an old house—all varying degrees of ugly. For many folks, however, wallpaper is decorating king: a relatively quick and easy way to add welcoming warmth.

Choices certainly abound; for kitchens, solid vinyl wallpapers are the better choice for scrubbability. If you're really gung-ho on the papering concept (or really uncertain about your choice), you may also want to look for a "strippable" brand that can be more easily removed in the future.

Wallpaper is sold in rolls that may be from 20 1/2 to 36 inches wide. When you calculate the amount to buy, remember to add a "fudge factor" of at least 10 percent to allow for matching of patterns, mistakes and cutting loss. (To minimize waste, look for patterns with a short "repeat.") When in doubt, err on the side of buying MORE than you need. Most stores will allow you to return unopened rolls, but you may find it difficult to locate the right pattern and exact dye lot if you find you need to purchase more paper a month from now. And it's always a good idea to have extra on hand for future repairs.

To prepare walls for papering, wash them thoroughly and let dry; remove switch-plate and outlet covers. With glossy paint or areas where grease has been a problem, you may want to use a TSP (trisodium phosphate) solution—which both etches the walls slightly and acts as an excellent de-greaser. Be sure to use gloves, and rinse thoroughly. Some experts also recommend painting with a special "primer/sizer" coat to promote adhesion. If you already have papered walls, you can paper over them but it's best to remove the old paper before beginning (rent a steamer at your paint store to make this daunting task a little easier). If you won't be papering the ceiling, consider repainting it now before you hang your new wallpaper.

Tip:
If you're using pre-pasted paper, wet the paper in a WARM water bath to help soften the glue faster. For unpasted papers, a sponge-type paint roller makes fast work of distributing the adhesive evenly.

**TIPS FROM
THE PROS:**

"If you hope to stay married, hanging wallpaper with your spouse is NOT a good idea. Frankly, I'd rather have the help of a small child … or maybe the family pet!"

—Lesley Morrison, wallpaper veteran

Begin at a point where a mismatch of patterns (the usual result by the time you run from start to finish around the room) will be least obvious—an out-of-the-way corner or a spot over a door or window are classic choices. Use a 6-foot level to draw a plumb floor-to-ceiling line to help get your first piece straight.

Cut each piece of paper about 4 inches too long, so you'll have 2 inches extra at the top and bottom. Hold at the top, and make sure that critical first edge goes on straight. Smooth the paper into place with a wallpaper brush. Once you have several sheets in place, trim off the excess lengths with a razor knife (a broad drywall knife makes a dandy straight-edge), and clean off any excess paste with a wet sponge. Strike edges once with a seam roller to flatten seams (don't repeat or you may leave a shiny spot!)

For turning-the-corner pieces, cut a strip that's wide enough to extend 1/2 inch past the corner, then use the cut remainder to begin the next wall. Since corners often aren't exactly plumb, chalk another plumb line to serve as a guide for the factory edge, allowing the cut edge to overlap the corner slightly; then trim for a precise fit.

Hang paper right over wall switches and outlet boxes; when you're done, turn the power off and carefully trim the paper in those areas back with a razor knife. Start with a small "X" in the center, and then carefully enlarge your cut.

Save any leftover lengths and large remnants to cover plastic switchplates and for future repairs.

If you're looking for only a splash of color and pattern, consider using just a wallpaper border. Installation is quick and easy; most border papers come pre-pasted, and little cutting is required. To make sure your first strip goes on straight, use a level to draw a horizontal pencil line as a guide, and check the distance between your line and the ceiling (or nearest horizontal surface) at several points to make sure your line is running true.

Molding & Gingerbread

Moldings, spindle-style spandrels, brackets and other "gingerbread" can add a hefty dash of architectural sizzle—all for a relatively nominal price. Home-improvement stores carry a wide range of stock molding and at least a handful of decorative accents; specialty catalogs and custom millworks offer more unusual styles and period reproduction designs.

Try adding a narrow "plate-rail" molding six to twelve inches below the ceiling; paint walls above the plate-rail a slightly lighter variation of the shade below to "raise" the ceiling and increase the sense of spaciousness.

Or install chair rail molding at one-third of the wall's height. Paint contrasting colors above and below the molding; or use wallpaper above and mimic traditional wainscoting below with tongue-and-groove planking or vertical grooved paneling.

Add a decorative crown molding at the top edge of your upper cabinets; attached carved wooden brackets below for a decorative flourish. Other architectural elements that can add flair and fun include Victorian-style "spandrels" (running "ladder"-style openwork), carved supports known as "corbels," and decorative brackets. Space a problem? Add a short length of "functional molding": a wooden Shaker peg rack for towels, mugs, measuring cups and spoons, or utensils.

Tiny strips of molding can also add a "paneled" look to simple cabinet faces or modern flat interior doors. Use a miter saw to cut molding strips to outline the shape desired; glue in place with construction adhesive or carpenter's wood glue (tack with finish nails or tape in place until dry).

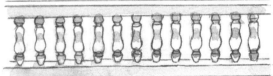

Spandrels

Corbel   Brackets

Hangups & Other Clever Gadgets & Gizmos

TIPS FROM THE PROS:

"We have one wall in the kitchen that's outfitted with pegboard where I hang my frying pans, saucepans, and so forth—we actually took out a window to provide the additional wall space. My husband drew outlines of all the pans, so it's easy to put them back in the right place."

—*Julia Child, author of The French Chef Cookbook (30th Anniversary edition, May 1998), and host of the television series "Master Chef" and "Baking at Julia's"*

A variety of simple add-ons can improve the storage options and function of an existing kitchen—without breaking the bank.

Hanging pot racks make a decorative virtue out of a limited-space necessity—and solve that ever-difficult problem of storing pots and pans within easy reach. Racks may be either wall- or ceiling-mounted; just make certain to anchor them securely in a stud or ceiling joist. Upscale versions include hooks that swivel, bright chrome finish or decorative cast-iron details.

For a cheery country look, consider suspending a small wooden ladder or other antique in place of the traditional pot rack frame. And don't limit your open-storage options to ordinary pots and pans; festoon your decorative display with antique miner's lanterns, bright copper cookware, hanging baskets, garlic braids and dried herb bouquets for added color, texture and interest.

Adding shelving is another easy and inexpensive way to increase storage space in your kitchen, and help keep counters clear of clutter. Consider adding a narrow shelf just below ceiling height to display canisters, jars, or other decorative collectibles. A short, narrow ledge might hold a clock, photos, or small-framed prints. For even more drama, add up-lighting or back-lighting.

One appliance manufacturer offers a clever (and inexpensive) plastic bracket that hangs from your refrigerator shelf to free up storage space while keeping that box of baking soda from tipping and spilling.

Other creative gadgets that can help keep you organized include "Lazy Susan" add-ons for both cupboards and inside your fridge. And if you're bugged by constantly reaching inside a cabinet for your trash container, there's now a clever device that slides the shelf toward you whenever you open the cabinet door.

TIPS FROM THE PROS:

"I like to hang my measuring cups and spoons up on the wall. They're used all the time; I keep several sets handy."

—Rose Levy Beranbaum, author of seven books, including *The Cake Bible* and *The Pie & Pastry Bible*

Message Center

Tired of wondering who Sandy went to visit after school, or what time batting practice is supposed to be?

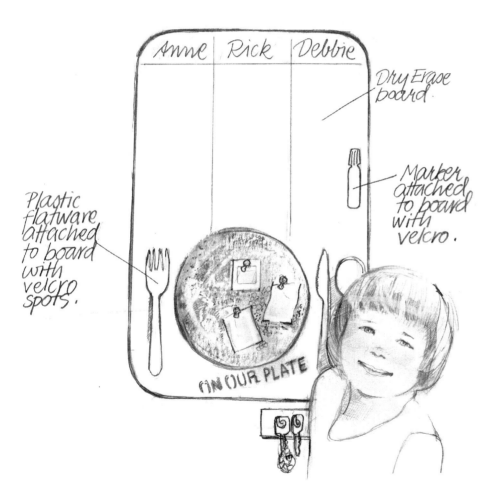

- ✎ It's easy to build your own "family message center."

- ✎ Paint a square of plywood or Masonite with spray-on "blackboard paint."

- ✎ Glue on a heart-shaped section of cork (or use a hot glue gun to attach an assortment of wine corks) for pushpin notes.

- ✎ keep chalk, pens and notepaper handy by attaching a small basket or wooden box as a "tray" at the bottom.

Facelifts on a Budget

Yes, you can work magic in your kitchen on a budget. Whether you're after a fresh new look or you just want to maximize your kitchen's usefulness, the solution could be as simple as adding a piece of furniture, or updating that funky faucet. Here's a range of fun facelift options—plus some choices to consider before you make that purchase.

Faucets

Maybe the chrome was long ago polished into oblivion. Maybe it's developed an annoying drip. Perhaps it's just plain ugly.

Hate your existing faucet? Installing a new one's a relatively painless project—unless you decide to do it yourself, anyway. (See "Faucet Follies," page 59.) For a few hundred bucks, you can jazz up your kitchen's look and make dishwashing chores more convenient.

Faucet options have come a long way since the days when the soap dish was built right in. Now, you can have your pick of chrome, brass, pewter or colored epoxy finishes—or even a dazzling combination. Choose from traditional 8- to 10-inch spout designs,

TIPS FROM THE PROS:

"People sometimes put those high, arching faucets on standard sinks and then find out that they splash. I have a simple, professional-style faucet that raises up if you need to fill a big pot or have a sink full of dishes—I've used this one for over 10 years and it's still working great. Sometimes I really think simple is better—whether it's faucets or practically anything else. When you go for fancy gadgets, there's more that can go wrong."

—*Rose Levy Beranbaum, author of The Pie and Pastry Bible*

or look for long-reach 12- or 14-inch styles. Some manufacturers offer what may be the best of both in compact units that feature pullout spouts—sort of an all-in-one version of the old-fashioned vegetable sprayer. (Just be sure to look for one that retracts easily.)

Other faucet-related options include a matching soap dispenser, or even a water-filtration system built right in. And if you love soups and stews but hate trying to wedge those oversize pots under your faucet for cleaning afterward, take heart. Adjustable faucets allow your spout to rise (literally) to the occasion. (Some pros swear by the professional models; check them out at a plumbing dealer or culinary supply store.)

Myself, I prefer the convenience of a single-handle faucet design. But you'll find a variety of styles to choose from, from super-sleek modern to radically retro. You can find genuine antique faucets at salvage shops and perhaps estate sales, but locating period plumbing parts to rebuild them can be, well, no small challenge. A number of manufacturers now offer vintage reproductions for that antique look without the antique drip.

When you shop for a new faucet, here's one hard-earned bit of plumbing wisdom: Do NOT buy cheap and expect quality. Sure, the styles may look similar. But bargain faucets won't last like the real thing. For no-hassle performance and a finish that won't flake out before your next birthday, choose a good name brand—and expect to pay for it. Read the box carefully before you buy; the "gold standard" for faucet durability is an all-brass inner body.

Remember to choose a model that will fit the number (and spacing) of the holes in your existing sink. A typical two-handled faucet will require three holes, with the outer two spaced 8 inches apart. A single-lever faucet may take one hole or three. And if you're purchasing a faucet with a separate sprayer attachment, you may need four holes. Be sure to read the box carefully before you buy to know how many holes are required. (Look underneath your existing sink with a flashlight, or ask your plumber to help you determine your sink's hole configuration.)

FAUCET FOLLIES: Do It Yourself?

Let's talk turkey here. . . or in this case, chicken. Yes, you probably CAN do anything you set your mind to—including changing a faucet. But what's involved may be more than you bargained for.

First, there are a variety of potential pitfalls just in loosening that old faucet from its mounting. Phrases like "rusted in place" and "rounded off threads" take on new meaning when you're lying on your back under a sink juggling a flashlight and tools. (If you do insist on trying this ungraceful dance, there's a specialized tool that can save you considerable swearing called a "basin wrench." Buy one before you begin!)

Then there are assorted problems you can run into with the water stops (those little handles under the sink that shut the water off) and water-supply lines. Old water stops may not close completely anymore, which means you'll have to shut the water off at the main—if you're lucky and that shut-off works. And just finding the correct replacement parts for stops and supply lines can be a major challenge. Standardization? Not in the plumbing industry. There are 1/2-inch parts, 3/8-inch parts, inside vs. outside diameters to consider, angled stops and straight stops, and screw-on vs. compression fittings. Have I discouraged you yet?

When you finally get to it, putting the new faucet in place should (and I emphasize "should") be the easy part. Just make sure that the faucet is sitting straight (and not backward), and that all connections are tight. If there's a leak, you get to try that last step again.

The bottom line: Good plumbers are worth every penny of their exorbitant hourly rates. Even if hiring a pro doubles the cost of your new faucet, remember ... it's still a bargain. The job will get done quicker. You won't be sporting five new gray hairs and a bruised scalp. Your kid won't embarrass you in public by repeating those "new words" he learned from Mommy.

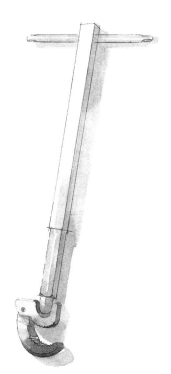

basin wrench

CAUTION:

If your home was built before 1980, your sheet flooring or tile squares may contain asbestos fibers in either the paper backing or the adhesive layer. When in doubt, have an expert evaluate your old tile before beginning any flooring project. A lab can usually analyze a small sample in less than a week for about $30 (tile and adhesive will count as two samples). Check your local Yellow Pages under "Asbestos Consulting & Testing." If your existing flooring materials are found to contain asbestos, discuss options for removal with asbestos-abatement professionals, or leave the existing floor in place and cover with new underlayment and finish materials.

If you've got more holes in the sink than you need, no problem. Extra holes are often covered by the faucet base, or can be capped with a special add-on piece. But if you don't have *enough* holes for the faucet you're planning to buy, or if the spacing is off, that could be a problem. If you've got a stainless steel sink, your plumber may be able to simply drill an extra hole. But with porcelain or cast-iron sinks, you'll probably need to replace the sink with one that will fit your new faucet.

Many manufacturers now offer special "anti-tarnish" finishes and "lifetime" warranties. But not all finishes—or warranties—are equal. Take a close squint at the fine print before you buy. What exactly is the manufacturer standing behind? Pay special attention to what is "limited" about that limited warranty, and what sort of documentation you will need to keep in order to make a claim.

Flooring

Sure, you could spend a small fortune on your kitchen floor. But a new look in flooring doesn't *have* to be expensive.

Vinyl flooring (also known as "resilient" tile) is today's most popular choice in kitchens and baths—and for good reason. It's easy on your feet *and* kind on your budget.

Vinyl comes in one-foot squares, or as rolled sheeting that's either 6 or 12 feet wide. Choose squares for easiest do-it-yourself installation; they can also be a great way to vary your floor's pattern with a checkerboard or border design. Most homeowner-type tile squares come with a convenient self-adhesive backing. In my experience, however, it's best to avoid the cheapest offerings on your home-improvement store shelves; ultra-thin vinyl tiles just don't last (and sometimes don't even stay stuck). Opt for thicker, higher-quality tiles.

Also an option: heavy-duty, commercial-grade tile squares. Instead of being self-stick, these usually require you to trowel on a thin layer of adhesive before laying the tile, but don't let that put you off; it's easy enough to do, and commercial tiles will give you excellent, long-lasting performance.

Sheet vinyl is a bit more difficult to install (okay, a *good* bit more difficult) than tile squares, but the more professional-looking results repay the extra time and trouble. Here again, opt for at least a medium-grade product—the cheapest "economy" sheet vinyl will give you more hassles than it's worth. Look for color that is deeply embedded in the product, rather than just printed on the surface. When in doubt, read the warranty. That's often a good clue to relative life expectancy when you're comparing products.

Thinking about installing new vinyl flooring on your own? Tile squares in particular make the job pretty simple, and doing it yourself can certainly save a good bit of money. Here are a few things for "D-I-Y"ers to keep in mind:

- Begin by carefully removing any wooden moldings or baseboards around the perimeter of the room, and pry up any metal threshold strips at doorways. Save what you can to re-install after the new vinyl is down.

- Vinyl floor tile (whether you're using squares or sheets) must be installed over a perfectly clean, smooth surface. *Don't* try to lay new vinyl over old; go ahead and remove the existing layer of vinyl or linoleum. This involves largely the "sweat" part of "sweat equity"; use a putty knife to get underneath and pry. You may be able to soften the old adhesive somewhat by heating the tile with a blow dryer, or by laying a soft, thin cloth on top and rubbing gently with an iron set on medium heat.

- For tile squares, find the exact center of the room. Lay out a test row running in both directions (like a "+" sign), and adjust your starting point to equalize the gaps at the edges. Chalk a straight line for a starter row. Carefully place the first tile along the lines you've marked, then continue laying tiles in a stair-step pattern.

Tip: For high-traffic households, you may want to pick a vinyl that will hide the dirt. Skip those sparkling (but unforgiving) whites in favor of deeper hues, and opt for the camouflage of busy or mottled patterns. While most vinyl flooring does have some surface texture, try to avoid styles with deep grooves or indentations that will collect and hold dirt.

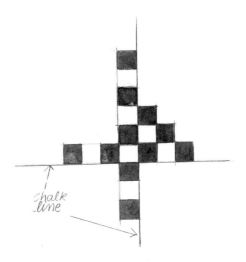

chalk line

• Start your perimeter "fill-in" pieces in the middle of a wall, then work toward either edge. To cut partial tiles, use stiff paper or cardboard as a template. Or transfer the needed dimension by laying the tile to be cut (with its paper backing still on) on top of the next full tile back from the wall. Use another tile as a guide to transfer the proper dimension by butting your guide tile tight up against the wall. Then simply mark where its back edge overlaps the tile to be cut. The piece still showing will be a perfect fit for the missing piece along the perimeter.

Tip:

Vinyl flooring is easiest to work with when it's warm. Allow your boxed tile or rolled sheet vinyl time to come up to room temperature before installing it.

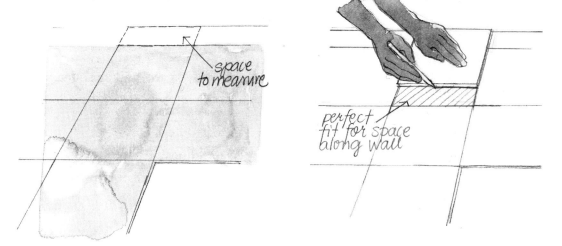

• Planning to install sheet vinyl instead? As a rule of thumb, this is *not* a task for D-I-Y beginners. Especially if your floor plan is complex or installation will require a seam, you may be happiest with the result if you simply pay a pro to do it. If you're still convinced you want to tackle the project yourself, a paper template can help you get the vinyl cut to the correct dimensions. Roll back half of the vinyl at a time, and trowel down a thin layer of adhesive. Work from the center outward.

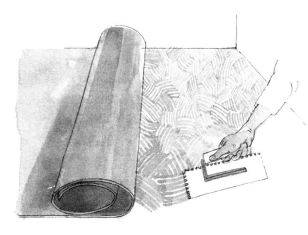

Laminate flooring, first introduced in the United States in 1994, is fast finding its own following. Made to resemble wood planking or stone, laminates are constructed by fusing a thin layer of real wood or a photographic look-alike onto a plywood or fiberboard base, and coating it with a protective finish coat for shine and durability.

With their tough, attractive, and easy-to-clean surface, it's little wonder laminates have become so popular. And though not quite as economical as vinyl (prices range from about $6 to $9 per square foot, installed), laminates are easier to install than the higher-end stone or solid-wood flooring they so closely resemble.

Laminates are sold as individual planks or prefabricated squares or rectangular sections. Some must be nailed or glued down; others are designed to snap together using a tongue-and-groove system that simply "floats" over the existing floor, with no special sub-floor adhesive required. Because products are modularized, you can often mix and match units from a single manufacturer (tiles with planks, or light and dark finishes, for example) to create a special border or pattern.

Wood laminates (sometimes called "engineered wood") do have some important differences from their plastic laminate cousins, beyond simply their exterior surface. Most plastic laminate products tend to be thinner—a plus if you're worried about raising existing floor levels. On the other hand, plastic laminates must be replaced when their wear layer is gone, while some (but not all) wood-laminate products can be refinished at least once in the future, if necessary.

Whatever type of laminate you choose, look for a product that's made to stand up to the traffic and occasional spills of kitchen use, and select one with at least a 10- to 15-year warranty. For extremely high-wear areas, commercial-grade products may offer better performance for a relatively small increase in price. Steer clear of extremely low-end laminates, which may warp or de-laminate.

Remember linoleum? Written off as a dowdy antique after vinyl flooring hit the market in 1947, this vintage material may now be making a comeback. Some 90 percent of linoleum sold in the U.S. today is used for commercial applications—a testimony in itself to the stuff's durability. But there's been a recent resurgence of interest in linoleum for residential use. In addition to wearing well, linoleum boasts natural anti-bacterial qualities and is produced from all-natural materials including cork, limestone, linseed oil, wood, and jute. Unlike the drab designs of yesteryear, today's lino comes in a wide range of zingy colors. Cost is roughly comparable to sheet vinyl. Squares of linoleum are easy enough for D-I-Yers. But leave the installation of sheet lino to professionals, as it requires special tools and techniques.

Backsplash

One of the most overlooked, underappreciated areas of a kitchen is the backsplash area—that blank expanse of wall just above your countertop. Yet because of its location, even a small addition of color or design is instantly eye-catching. And best of all, a backsplash makeover can be one of the fastest and most economical of kitchen upgrades.

The possibilities are nearly endless: Add an expanse of lively wallpaper, or stencil in a trailing vine; create a wash of bright salmon or lemon-yellow and stud with hooks for kitchen utensils; cover the area with thin squares of stone, Mexican primitive tiles, or metal-glazed ceramic tile for a hammered-copper look.

Many backsplash options make relatively easy do-it-yourself projects. If you decide to tackle one yourself, here are a few pointers:

- Remember that although a backsplash is generally not a high-wear area, it is subject (as the name implies) to splashes and moisture. Consider protecting delicate stencils and faux-finish paints with a clear acrylic topcoat for easy cleaning.

- Planning to mount a cup hook, a towel holder, or a spice rack? Make sure you use the proper fastener for the job. There are special fasteners made expressly for use with drywall, plaster, tile, or masonry, and to provide light-, medium-, and heavy-duty support. Ask a knowledgeable salesperson at your local hardware store to help you find a suitable fastener.

plastic anchor

E-Z anchor

hollow wall anchor

toggle bolt

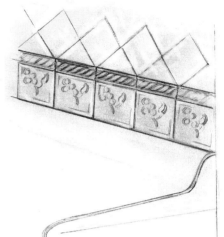

- A row or two of ceramic tile can dress up even the most ordinary laminate countertop. Consider tiling your entire backsplash area to make it an even bigger design element of your kitchen.

  Note: It's easy enough to chip away and replace any existing wall tiles; but if your backsplash is a molded laminate formed in one piece with your countertop, it's probably better to simply install tile above the existing laminate backsplash. While it is possible to cut laminate, you run the risk of splintering the finish at the cut edge.

- To be thrifty, select ordinary white or stock color tile; add a few more-expensive tiles as focal points if you wish. Or opt for extravagant and choose imported or hand-painted tile. While these will run considerably more, you may find the bottom line still quite acceptable since the area you're covering is limited.

Refinishing & Refacing Cabinets

Like your existing cabinets, but hate the three coats of paint or chipped varnish they're sporting? Consider refinishing. Though stripping, sanding, and applying multiple coats of a new finish is labor-intensive, you can do it yourself. Or hire a professional—check the Yellow Pages under "Furniture Repair & Refinishing," "Kitchen Cabinets," or "Cabinetmakers." Prices will vary depending on where you live and what you're having done, but professional refinishing may cost as little as 20 or 25 percent of what new cabinets would run. Expect the entire project to take one to three weeks.

Another option you may want to look into is cabinet refacing. In this slightly more complicated procedure, new doors and drawer fronts are built to the exact sizes of your existing openings, and a matching veneer is applied over the cabinet's frame. Most home-

improvement centers can order the materials and connect you with a local contractor to do the work. For roughly half the cost of replacement, you'll get a whole new look. "Up and extra" options include stylish leaded-glass panels, crown moldings, and self-closing or Euro-style hinges. Once parts arrive, the work can often be completed in less than a week.

Freestanding Furniture

When we think of kitchen furniture, most often it's of boring standbys like a dinette and chairs. But the creative use of furniture—including things not usually found in the kitchen—can provide a variety of convenient, useful storage and work space. And best of all, if there's a move in your future, you CAN take it with you when you go!

Furniture doesn't have to be large to be a huge asset in the kitchen. Move telephone clutter off your countertop with a convenient phone table/magazine rack. Consider a rolling TV-style cart for (yes) a little kitchen entertainment while you're fixing the next fine meal (cookbooks and recipe boxes may fit perfectly on a lower shelf). Small, simple storage cabinets or assemble-yourself open shelving can accommodate canned goods, a wine rack, or even heavy mixers and other appliances when not in service.

Desperate for extra work room but stuck with a kitchen where space is tight? Some mail-order sources offer maple-laminated tables on stainless steel legs in sizes as small as 2' square. Or look for drop leaf-style work carts whose arms will tuck out of the way when not in use.

If you're blessed with a bit of extra wall space, a handy hutch can become a "kitchen armoire" to house a microwave or store linens, while its glass-fronted doors display dishes or pottery.

Tip:

Got a flair for do-it-your-self? A wide variety of furniture now comes "ready to assemble"—at prices 20 to 40 percent less than what you'd pay for comparable products on a showroom floor. Precision engineering and some clever fastener design have simplified assembly. And many manufacturers include toll-free help lines in case you get stuck.

Rolling bookcase units designed for the living room can make great "keepers" for the kitchen as well. Try using one as a room divider that can be wheeled out of the way when company comes. An oak wine rack can also double as a stylish way to separate spaces.

Contemplating adding a center "island"? Try an antique (or antique-look) sideboard with a marble top as a practical—and beautiful—alternative. Or get a double bang for the bucks with a tallish 37-inch kitchen worktable that can double as a breakfast bar. Commercial kitchen-supply stores offer a variety of wonderful, portable, rolling islands with wood, stone, or stainless steel work surfaces. Larger ones may have hooks on the side to hang pots or utensils, plus handy shelves on the bottom for those difficult-to-store oversize pots. If you choose a kitchen work island on wheels, just be certain they lock firmly into place.

Details, Details

Does your refrigerator open the most convenient way? Or are you constantly walking around the door to put something in or take things out?

Okay, so it's not the sexiest change you could make to your kitchen. But if you've got a relatively modern refrigerator, changing the direction the doors open is certainly one of the least expensive changes you can make—grab a few basic tools, and it won't cost you a penny. And this simple switch can make a huge, functional difference in how your kitchen works and feels.

Here's the trick: On most modern refrigerators, the handles and hinges are made to be easily swapped. Pop off the plastic cover over the hinge mechanism on top of your freezer door. Underneath you'll find the hinge plate held in place with a series of screws (some may have hexagonal heads that require a nut-driver to remove). Open the doors, and you'll find similar mounting brackets holding the top and bottom of your main refrigerator door. Door handles simply unscrew. Mounting holes are identical on both the left and right of your fridge, so handles and brackets can be easily swapped to the other side (you may need to pop out plastic concealer buttons to find the holes). And voila!

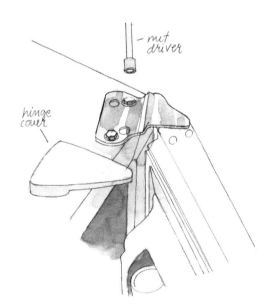

"I took a board, hinged it, cut a couple of slots in the middle, and attached it to my central work table/chopping block to hold my knives. It's a simple and convenient arrangement—though obviously practical only for those of us who don't have kids! When you buy knives, by the way, go to a professional restaurant equipment place and buy good ones. They're made to be used over and over instead of once a month."

—Ann Cooper, corporate chef

Small-Space Solutions

Is your kitchen just a little short on space? Flat-out tiny? Hardly bigger than the proverbial breadbox? Fear not. Here are some suggestions that can help you find a smidgen of "extra" room in the snuggest layout and make the most of the space you've got.

Retrieving "Lost" Space

Where to look to find underutilized space? Start by "clearing the deck" on your countertops. A few chatchkas here, a handful of knick-knacks there, and before you know it you've got a beautifully decorated kitchen—with absolutely no room in which to work.

In my own kitchen, we rediscovered the most useful counter space of all—an L-shaped corner—under a somewhat droopy plant. The greenery found a more appropriate home beside a living room window, and all of us were immensely happier. Sounds obvious, doesn't it? But it took a helpful suggestion from a friend before we, er, saw the light.

Once you've created a little elbowroom on your counters, it's time to tackle the *inside* of your cabinets. The prime culprit there is unused "head room"—shorter items

TIPS FROM THE PROS:

"Sometimes I think the best way to deal with a tiny cramped kitchen is to completely surrender to the spatial dharma of it all. By that I mean really clutter it up! Turn it into a diorama of your life with pictures, chatchkas, dried flowers, cat toys, funky refrigerator magnets—a visual festival, an open treasure chest. Or, on the opposite end of the spectrum, you can go really stark: remove everything from all surfaces, do nothing more than boil water for tea, and commit to ordering lots of take-out."

—Meredith Gould, author of *Working At Home*

like spice containers with lots of dead air space above them. The solution: if your shelves are adjustable, raise or lower them to better fit their contents. Or double up, using two-tiered wire organizers. Also consider moving very short items like spices to a spot all their own—if you haven't already discovered the "miracle" of the spice drawer, give it a shot!

You may also discover a wealth of unused space on *vertical* surfaces. Hooks or shallow racks can help make use of the interior walls and door backs of cupboards, for example. What to store there? The list is virtually endless. Hang an extra set of measuring spoons; tuck away wraps, bags, pot lids or even spices.

Think vertical when it comes to wall areas, as well. Open shelves can be simply beautiful—and beautifully practical. Tuck a narrow shelf below your wall cabinets, or make the most of an out-of-the-way corner with a free-standing metal baker's rack. And when you're considering spots for extra shelving, don't forget to look UP. A shelf circling the room just below ceiling height could hold little-used serving dishes, for example. Or let a shelf display decorative baskets, pottery, tins and other collectibles.

Before and after

TIPS FROM THE PROS:

"TVs, phones, books, decorative knick-knacks and rarely used small appliances—get rid of all the countertop nonsense. While others focus on the esoterica of beautiful kitchens, I'm into less clutter, and function over form. I'm no fan of paper towels, so they're the first to disappear. Oh, and those wooden dish racks people seem so fond of these days? Kindling!"

—Ann F. Potter, independent private chef, San Antonio, Texas

Getting Organized

Does the mere thought of tackling your Tupperware drawer make you hyperventilate? You're not alone. From spare batteries to that unwieldy collection of empty butter tubs, kitchen clutter has a way of accumulating slowly ... almost imperceptibly, until it's hard to imagine life without it.

The two cardinal rules for kitchen organizing: First, take everything out. Then get ruthless—or get help. Enlist the dispassionate eye of a faithful friend (you can always promise to help with her kitchen next weekend).

Here are a few additional organizing tips to help you get started:

- ✎ There's a place for everything—but that place is not necessarily in the kitchen. Don't waste valuable drawer or counter space on items that really belong elsewhere. Move bills, correspondence, and other paper clutter to a central bill-paying station or office; store table linens in your linen closet or dining area; collect hardware items like hammer, pliers and nails in a tool tote in the garage; shift once-a-year holiday dishes and rarely used appliances to a pantry or utility closet.

- ✎ Plan on spending a little to save a lot—a lot of time and energy searching, that is. Go ahead. Splurge on drawer organizers, Lazy Susans, snap-together trays, cabinet stackers, and cut-to-fit dividers. It'll probably set you back less than a fancy dinner out (okay, maybe two fancy dinners) and will make your life easier for years to come.

TIPS FROM THE PROS:

"Don't keep your spices near an oven! Those fancy countertop spice racks look nice, but when delicate herbs and spices are exposed to heat and light, they have a much shorter life. Try one of those clever drawer racks instead."

—*Rose Levy Beranbaum,* author of *The Cake Bible* and *The Pie and Pastry Bible*

- Use it—or lose it. You probably won't miss the vintage fondue pot collecting dust in the back of your cupboard or that mug with the handle missing—honest. If you haven't used a kitchen item in the past year, or if it's chipped, broken, or well past the "use by" date, GET RID of it. Can't bear to throw something away? Donate it to a worthy charity, drop it off at a local consignment shop, or schedule a garage sale.

- Use "premium space" wisely: Store most frequently used dishes and ingredients where they're easiest to reach. If you have to bend over, shove things out of the way, or stand on a step stool to reach something, make sure it's an item you don't use every day.

- Store items by task. Group baking needs together; keep cutlery near your dining table and pots and pans near the range; save steps by storing dishes within easy reach of the dishwasher or sink.

- Sometimes more IS better. Consider keeping duplicate sets of measuring cups and spoons where you use them most—in your baking area and near the sink, for example.

"If you do any pastry work at all, I'd recommend finding a slab of marble that's the right size to fit into the refrigerator, and keeping it there. If you turn it upside down, you can store other things right on top of it, and the surface stays clean. Then when you're doing pie dough or pastry, you can simply pull it out and it's pre-chilled—for pastry, that makes all the difference."

—*Julia Child*, author of *The French Chef Cookbook* (30th Anniversary edition, May 1998), and host of the television series "Master Chef" and "Baking at Julia's"

End Cookbook Clutter!

It may be a time-honored tradition—but the kitchen counter with its inevitable dust, dirt, flour, and grease is probably the worst place to keep your precious cookbook collection (And we won't even talk about the workspace it eats up).

Best of all, there are usually lots of other practical options. Is there an out-of-the-way shelf available in your pantry? How about space for a bookcase in an adjoining room or hallway? If possible, keep cookbooks close to the desk or work area where you prepare menus and grocery lists.

Invest in a stand that can hold the cookbook you're using upright (and as nearly as possible, out of harm's way!) while you're working from it.

"When you're organizing your kitchen, keep kids' activities in mind. When my kids were small, we kept measuring cups, spoons, soft toys, and books—things that preschoolers could do—on a lower shelf of a kitchen bookcase. That way they had 'their' play area in the kitchen, while I was working at the counter."

—Joan Stanford, co-owner of The Stanford Inn, Mendocino, California

Re-Design With Space In Mind

Consider these space-saving design classics:

✎ "Banquettes" are back—and for good reason. Using built-in benches takes up less room than the traditional dinette, maximizing seating space in cramped quarters. And with a little forethought, they can also provide under-seat storage.

✎ Widen an existing countertop to create an overhang. A ledge of as little as 6 or 8 inches may allow you to belly up with barstools.

✎ Check out "apartment-size" models at your appliance store. A compact refrigerator, for example, may hold plenty of groceries for a one- or two-person household, while allowing a few crucial extra inches for countertop and cabinets. Where space is really at a premium (and gourmet cooking isn't), ask about an "all-in-one" unit that combines sink, mini-fridge, and two gas burners, in one compact unit—the kind that offices or motels sometimes use.

✎ Stretch kitchen workspace with drop-leaf tables, pull-out cutting boards, and other "temporary" surfaces that can be pressed into service when needed, and folded away when not in use.

Pantry Makeover

If you're lucky enough to have a pantry, you know how utterly useful they can be—and how terribly tough to keep organized!

As with cupboards, the key to keeping your pantry ship-shape is to have a place for everything—and everything VISIBLY in its place. Store taller items in back; use stepped stackers and wire mini-shelves to optimize your use of space and to help make sure you can SEE each item.

Pullout wire basket organizers (the kind used in clothes closets) can be an extremely helpful pantry addition. Or simply use wicker baskets to hold napkins and other smaller items.

TIP:

If you don't have a formal pantry, consider adding a tall pantry cabinet in your garage, laundry area, or mudroom. Or ask a carpenter to create a niche for canned goods on the back of a door.

Where possible, group related items together. You may want to allocate one shelf exclusively to canned drinks, extra tea and coffee tins, and powdered beverage mixes, for example. Or perhaps you'll find it helpful to store pastas and canned tomato products together. There's no one right way to organize, of course; any system that makes sense to you will work. Just take your time and think it through. Storing items based on logical association will help you find what you're looking for quickly and easily, and help make it obvious where things should go when it's time to put away groceries.

Some folks also relegate little-used appliances to their pantry, rather than wasting prime cabinet space on them. One word of caution, however: Don't store heavy appliances on a high shelf, where they could fall and hurt you.

Storage for Pots & Pans

Hanging pot racks are a creative solution to that ever-difficult problem of storing pots and pans within easy reach.

Depending on the design of your pot rack, there may be room to store pot lids on a top shelf. Lids can also be hung on the inside face of cabinet doors, tucked in a deep drawer, or corralled in a wicker or plastic catch-all basket.

Yet another solution for the pots-and-pans dilemma: open shelving beneath a center island or worktable. This is a particularly attractive place to store large kettles or especially heavy cookware you'd prefer not to hang—no rooting around in the back of a corner cabinet.

TIPS FROM THE PROS:

"Serious home cooks should consider buying in bulk to save time and money. Most restaurant-supply companies sell to the public and have great square containers in all sizes, which are perfect for storing bulk food purchases—flour, sugar, grains and rice, etc. Little bottles of this and that drive me crazy, especially if they're products people use often."

—Ann F. Potter, independent private chef, San Antonio, Texas

Fixtures With Splash

They're the workhorses of any kitchen. But whether the particular beast that you're contemplating adding to your stable is a sink, disposal, oven, fridge or dishwasher, chances are it's undergone a significant design change—and features upgrade—in the last few years.

Today's fixtures are flexible—and often surprisingly colorful. Stock appliance colors routinely include not only the ever-popular white and almond, but also off-white and black. A stainless finish—extremely popular right now in ranges—is making the transition to dishwashers and other appliances, as well. And colored appliance panels are available for some brands in more than 50 dazzling hues.

Marketers tout not only new style and design features, but new standards for performance as well: Virtually all gas ranges now feature pilotless ignition, and faster-cooking ovens and snappy microwave/convection combinations are popping up in many manufacturers' lines. New "smart features" include time-delayed cooking settings, special extra-low burner options, and humidity-controlled refrigerator bins. And high-tech choices are getting more sophisticated all the time.

When shopping for any fixture or appliance, remember to compare more than simply price and features. Ask before you buy about the product's warranty, whether delivery and installation assistance are available (and how much they will cost), and where you'll

TIPS FROM THE PROS:

"I have a feeling that with all those television chefs and cooking videos now available, we will soon get used to having video or monitors in the kitchen where we can watch and get recipes. And there is going to be more intelligence built into the kitchen itself. In the next 10 years or so, your refrigerator will read the bar-codes on all the products inside so you'll know what you have and don't have, and what your shopping list will be."

—Jane Langmuir, adjunct associate professor, Rhode Island School of Design and Project Director for "Unlimited by Design"

**TIP FROM
THE PROS:**

*"Some people spend way
too much on equipment
they barely use. It's important to honestly assess
your needs before plunking
down a small fortune just
to keep up with the
Joneses. A state-of-the-
art trophy kitchen won't
make you a great chef! I
cook two meals a day for
my family on a four-burn-
er—who needs an eight-
burner monster to warm
canned soup and hotdogs
for the kids?"*

—*Ann F. Potter, independent private chef, San Antonio, Texas*

be able to obtain service and/or parts in the future. Also pay attention to energy efficiency ratings; those standardized yellow stickers help make comparison easier by clearly flag-
ging the average annual cost to operate each appliance.

Eager sales "assistants" may try to push you toward models loaded with ups and
extras by noting that the added cost is small when amortized over the lifetime of the appliance. And yes, it may pay to upgrade ...
IF you'll really use those features.

Similarly, it may pay to ask about
"package" prices on more than one appliance
if you're really planning to acquire a brand-
new everything. But don't let fast-talking
salesfolk sell you on a terrific five-appliance
deal if all you really need is a toaster oven.

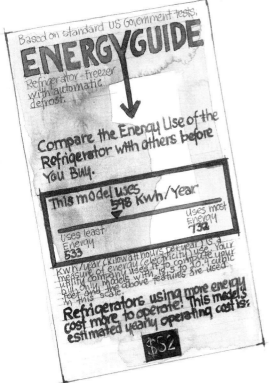

Appliance Checklist

Shopping for a new appliance? Here are some things you may want to consider:

- ✔ Do you want a freestanding or a built-in model? Freestanding units are often less expensive, and they're easier to replace if you decide to upgrade in the future.
- ✔ How important are quiet-operation features?
- ✔ Look for models designed for easy cleanup (seamless surfaces, flush installation). The fewer ledges, indentations, knobs, and seams, the easier the appliance will be to wipe clean.
- ✔ Check the controls—are they intuitive to use? Can you tell in a glance what's on and what's off?
- ✔ What size limitations are you working with? Keep in mind not only the width and height of the appliance itself, but also the clearances needed for appliance doors and handles. A side-by-side style refrigerator, for example, may require extra inches in width to allow doors (and inner drawers) to open fully. And don't forget to measure access dimensions. Will your whiz-bang new range need to fit through your front door and slide around three corners before it makes it to your kitchen?
- ✔ What plumbing or electrical work will be required to complete the installation? If you're switching from an electric to a gas range or adding an ice-on-the-door-style fridge in place of a non-ice-making model, you may need to hire an electrician and/or plumber. (Caution: work performed by a nonprofessional may void the manu- facturer's warranty.)

**TIPS FROM
THE PROS:**

"It's a good idea to pur-
chase your new sink early in
the remodeling process, so
your plumber, cabinet-
maker and tile guy can plan
accordingly. Never, ever,
make the actual counter-
top cut for the sink without
the template provided by
the sink manufacturer in
hand. Remember that for
special-order countertop
materials such as stone or
solid-surfacing, you'll need
to provide exact sink specifications to your fabricator
ahead of time."

—Michael Pantano, FCSI, commercial kitchen planner, president
of the Foodservice Consultants'
Society International, and partner in Culinary Advisors, a commercial foodservice facility planning firm

Sinks

Remember when sinks came in one color—white? In the good old, bad old days, sinks were made using a porcelain enamel coating over a cast-iron base and lasted seemingly forever. (Of course, if no one ever changed them, it was also because they were too heavy to move!)

Porcelain-enameled cast iron is still the tried-and-true choice for a heavy-duty, high quality sink, and today it's available in a rainbow of colors. It's exceptionally long-wear-ing although the finish, of course, can chip under a heavy direct blow. In general, the thicker the porcelain, the better the quality.

For a similar look with a somewhat more affordable price tag, you may want to consider a porcelain enamel sink with a steel base. Porcelain-on-steel sinks offer the same attractive, high-gloss finish, and they're significantly less heavy to install—some boast they are just half the weight of their cast-iron counterparts. But the porcelain enamel fin-ish is also thinner on steel sinks—only about 6 to 8 mils (thousandths of an inch) vs. 45 to 50 mils on cast iron—so it may be a bit more prone to chipping.

Sinks are now also manufactured from a variety of natural and synthetic materials. Some are made from the same material as solid-surfacing countertops. Others are formed from tiny chips or particles of natural stone (generally quartz or granite), bound together with a scratch- and stain-resistant resin. Advantages include high durability (no surface coat-ing to chip through), easy cleaning and a wide range of colors. Composites can offer the "look and feel" of a ceramic finish, and they boast excellent heat and stain resistance. For cooks who prefer the all-in-one-piece design, molded solid-surfacing materials such as Corian make possible a seamless sink/countertop option with a drain board molded right in.

Once the ugly duckling or institutional option, utilitarian stainless is again coming into its own, thanks in part to recent design interest in high-tech and commercial-look

kitchens. Combining remarkable durability with comparatively low cost and easy maintenance, stainless steel sinks also offer the practical virtue of deeper bowls than their non-
metal cousins. Manufacturers are quick to note that the metal surface won't chip, crack,
rust, burn, or stain, and brushed-style finishes help hide scratches and everyday wear.
With so many appealing features, it's little wonder that stainless steel is the sink material
of choice for an estimated 75 percent of consumers.

When shopping for a stainless steel sink, make sure you compare the gauge of the
metal; sinks that LOOK virtually identical (other than the price tag) may not be! Put
them to the "thump" test: the dead give-away to a thinner, lower-quality sink is a tinny-
sounding ring. But keep in mind that gauge numbers function in REVERSE: the lower
the gauge number, the thicker the material (and hence the more durable the sink). To
ensure good corrosion-resistance, look for a product with at least 8 percent nickel composition. ("18/8" on a box or label means the sink contains 18 percent chromium and 8
percent nickel). And be sure your sink has an insulating coating on the bottom to help
deaden sound and keep water hot longer. Brushed finishes are eminently practical, as they
hide tiny scratches. Unless you plan to buff your sink daily, stay away from shiny surfaces
that will only accentuate wear marks and fingerprints.

Once you've chosen the composition of your new sink, you'll still have some important decisions to make. One of the most critical questions is how your new sink will be
mounted. Are your cabinets designed to accommodate a self-rimming or drop-in style
sink? Do you need a model with a "tile-mount" edge to sit flush with the adjacent tile
surface? Or perhaps you plan to replace your entire countertop and want to switch to a
sink with the new no-lip, under-counter mounting style? (Several words of caution before
you choose this latter option: unless perfectly sealed, the countertop's cutout edge can
allow water to seep into the plywood substrate. Also inquire about installation technique
before you purchase an under-counter-mounted sink to be sure it won't be a problem to
REPLACE it in the future.)

TIP:

If possible, select a sink
large enough to wash cookie
sheets, and deep enough to
accommodate your biggest
stockpot. If you use large
cookware frequently, con-
sider choosing one large
bowl instead of a conven-
tional double sink.

Unraveling the Porcelain Enamel Mystery

If you find the term "porcelain enamel" a bit confusing when it comes to sinks, you're not alone. After all, you've probably seen those words applied to porcelain figurines and enamel house paints; porcelain toilets and fingernail enamels—many of which bear little resemblance to each other.

Sink manufacturers don't make it much easier to sort out the confusion. Depending on the particular maker, finishes may be described as "enamel," "porcelain," or even "porcelain enamel."

Luckily, the bottom line is that, at least when it comes to sinks, all of those terms mean essentially the same thing: a glass coating material that's sifted or sprayed onto a metal base, and then fired to bond them together. (As for fingernail enamel and enamel house paints—well, those are obviously completely different animals!)

Among the many types of porcelain enamel sinks on the market, there are important differences you should know about, however. First and foremost, the type of preformed metal base over which the glass coating is applied may be either cast iron or steel. Ingredients in the glass coating will vary slightly to match the "thermal expansion properties" (expansion and contraction) of the underlying metal. The thickness of the porcelain enamel coating will also differ; the glass coating over sheet steel is thinner than that applied over cast iron. And finally, the temperature at which the coating is fired (to fuse the glass to the metal) will vary slightly from approximately 1,600 to 1,650 degrees Fahrenheit, depending on the chemical composition of the glass coating material and whether the metal base is iron or steel.

You may have heard rumors that the porcelain enamel coating on cast iron sinks is no longer as tough and chip-resistant as it once was, now that lead has been removed from the glaze. Not so, according to industry experts.

"Lead-free enamels for cast iron are every bit as durable as their leaded predecessors," confirms Porcelain Enamel Institute spokesman Cullen Hackler. "For cast-iron sinks, what the removal of lead has done is to change the look of the finish slightly. Coatings with a high lead content tend to have more depth—think about the brilliance you find in fine lead crystal, for example. Even after lead was removed as an ingredient in recent years, the porcelain enamel industry has made tremendous strides in reducing chipping while preserving color and opacity. And research and development continues in the industry that will help make porcelain enamel coatings even more flexible and durable in the future."

The folks at Kohler also say they've done extensive mechanical and chemical testing, and confirm that "getting the lead out" has not seriously impaired durability for their porcelain enamel sinks. "Our new lead-free formula did require a slight trade-off between making the product acid-resistant or alkali-resistant," explains Elisabeth Sutton, Kohler's marketing manager for kitchen products. "We felt it was more important to emphasize alkali-resistance because soap is used so much around sinks. So if you regularly dump acid foods like orange juice in your sink and don't rinse with water, it could cause a slight etching effect over a long period of time. But the actual difference in acid-resistance between the old and the new porcelain formulas is so slight it's nearly imperceptible."

Bowl arrangements are now as varied as the manufacturers' imaginations. In addition to the standard two-bowl divided sink, you can now choose "bowl-and-a-half" styles; "triple" bowl sinks with the middle depression featuring a garbage disposal; or an angled corner arrangement. The old-fashioned country-kitchen look with an "apron front" is also making a comeback with some kitchen designers. And if you're really tickled by "custom" options, some manufacturers now offer made-to-fit accessories such as cutting board, dish drain, and colander.

If your space—and budget—permits, consider the virtues of including more than one sink in your kitchen design. You may find a second, smaller sink useful near a food preparation area or center island, for example. (Remember, of course, that you'll have to run additional plumbing!)

Disposal

In the garbage disposal game, horsepower is the trump card. Look for a disposal motor rated for at least 1/2 horsepower; a unit that provides 3/4, 1, or perhaps even 1.5 hp is even better.

New models may include a "reverse" function. As a safety measure, some also feature a lid-activated design that prevents activating the disposer unless the lid is in place.

If your kitchen already includes a garbage disposal, the basic plumbing and wiring needed to serve the disposal will already be in place. If you don't presently have a disposal, however, adding one can be a bit of a project. You'll need to run wiring for the on/off switch, tap into the drain, and add a hose to connect the disposal to your dishwasher. Ask a plumber to assess your current setup and give you a bid.

Ranges, Cooktops & Ovens

Let's start with the basics: whether it's a new range, cooktop or oven, the first decision you'll need to make is whether to choose a gas or an electric model.

The race is closer than it used to be. Although gas used to be the hands-down choice for many cooks because of its rapid heat availability, recent innovations help some electric models to heat up significantly faster than they used to.

Gas appliances remain considerably cheaper to operate than their electric counterparts. And energy-saving pilotless ignition can help save even more; once an option, pilotless ignition is now required on gas ranges and ovens that come equipped with an electric cord.

Still, electric models often cost a bit less up front—perhaps one reason why a surprising 58 percent of American households today cook with electricity. And electric ranges are generally much easier to install (provided, of course, that the necessary plug-in connection is already there.)

Back to basics again: what type of power do you currently HAVE in your kitchen? Changing over from a gas-powered appliance to an electric model may require installing a 220-volt outlet—and potentially upgrading your electrical service. Similarly, it may be

Ever wonder who invented the garbage disposal? This ingenious device has a longer history than you might imagine.

According to one manufacturer's Web site, architect John W. Hammes created the first disposal in 1927 to make life a little easier for his wife. In 1938, Hammes began manufacturing his new invention, selling a modest 50 disposals. By 1960 the company he founded, In-Sink-Erator, boasted sales of 750,000 units, and today the company produces more than 3 million of Hammes' clever invention every year.

Source: http://www.insinkerator.com/Homeowner/about.html

According to the U.S. Department of Energy, choosing a gas oven with an electronic ignition can cut oven energy consumption by 40 percent (or, for a gas cooktop, 53 percent) compared to a pilot-flame model.

TIPS FROM THE PROS:

"I worked for people in New York who had these wonderful townhouses which were beautifully decorated. But they were spending all this money on stuff that just wasn't practical. You can't just buy a commercial 6-burner range and expect your ordinary home ventilation system to keep up with it—it's not going to work. And if your kitchen is on the third floor, that's a lot of weight on floor joists that probably weren't designed for it! Then too, when you use a restaurant-quality range and oven, the BTUs they put out are huge; you can't put out a fire with just baking soda or a mini fire extinguisher. You'll need to install a professional type of fire-suppression system."

—Ann F. Potter, independent private chef, San Antonio, Texas

costly to switch over to a gas appliance if there's not already a gas line in place where you need it.

Next on the decision tree, you'll need to decide whether to separate your oven from your stovetop. On the plus side, separating these functions allows you to spread out your work area so your cooktop can be located close to a prep area while hot ovens can be tucked away, out of your primary traffic pattern. The downside, however, is that wall-mounted ovens eat up potential countertop space. In cramped quarters, the compact, old-fashioned range is often the most space-saving solution.

Ranges   Standard width for most "plain vanilla" ranges is 30". Whether you choose a gas or electric model, most manufacturers offer a wide variety of colors, prices, and quality in freestanding, slide-in, or drop-in styles.

Think a self-cleaning oven is a luxury? Think again. The extra insulation provided in self-cleaning models may actually save you money on your normal cooking energy costs—unless you use the self-cleaning feature more than about once a month.

Not long ago, professional ranges were all the rage. These offered more (and more-powerful) burners and a wider cooking surface—up to a whopping 60 inches.

Though beautiful to look at and a dream to cook on, the downsides of truly professional ranges quickly became apparent. Because they're extremely heavy and not insulated for home applications, commercial ranges require extra-special measures for installation and venting. Factor in the costs of constructing a firewall, reinforcing your floor, installing a larger gas line, and adding a commercial hood and fire-suppression measures, and you can quickly see why the blush left the rose—or in this case, the range—for many homeowners.

Manufacturers took note, however, and quickly rallied to the rescue with lines of commercial-LOOK appliances. Today you can purchase high-style, high-performance models in 40, 45, 48, even 60" models that offer all the functionality of their commercial brothers, but are specially engineered for residential use; most require no special exhaust vents or expensive fire-suppression systems.

That's the good news. Or is it? Sure, these monumental ranges can handle big pots with aplomb. But they also demand a considerable amount of space. Make sure you REALLY have the oversize cookware or cooking needs to warrant such an investment, and pay extra attention to planning clearances and traffic patterns around an oversize range.

TIPS FROM THE PROS:

"In Feng Shui, the ancient Chinese art of placement, the stove is a symbol of the family's finances. Auspicious positioning of the stove can help determine the amount and quality of the family's cash flow. The best position for the stove is away from the entrance to the kitchen, and where the cook's back is not facing the entrance door. If this is not possible, simply placing a mirror on the wall above the stove will create the same results."

—Helen Jay, author of *Paper Dragons: Journey to the Shamanic Roots of Feng Shui* and co-director of the Feng Shui Designs Learning Center in Nevada City, California

What's New In Ranges

Used to be, a self-cleaning oven feature was "the" hot ticket in ranges. Today's models include a wide range of innovative options. Features to consider include:

- ✔ Sealed-burner construction

- ✔ Solid-surface cooktop (look for helpful "indicator" lights that show when a burner is on or remains hot)

- ✔ Variable BTU-burners

- ✔ Interchangeable units, including simmer plates, wok rings, grill or griddle options, and "bridge" burners than combine for larger heating area

- ✔ "Dual fuel" options such as gas-burner cooktop paired with an electric convection oven

- ✔ Infrared broiling

- ✔ Tilt-able control panel

- ✔ Child lockout feature

- ✔ Preheating buzzer that sounds when desired temperature is reached

Cooktops Cooktops themselves—whether freestanding or incorporated into a range unit—have also come a long way in recent years.

Again, the longstanding favorite fuel is gas. But more recently, manufacturers have come up with some exciting electric-powered options as well.

Among electric cooktops, the traditional, red-glowing coil type is the most basic—and least-expensive—option. Solid- or ceramic-surface designs also may incorporate a radiant (coil) burner, or may conceal quicker-to-heat halogen bulbs.

Yet another option for solid-surface cooktops is a heat unit that uses magnetic induction to produce heat in the pan itself, rather than in the cooktop's surface. (One caveat: Cooking utensils must be a ferrous material, i.e., made of iron, to produce this magnetically induced heat, so glass or aluminum cookware will not work on these stovetops.)

And for those who just can't make up their mind (or insist on the best of both worlds!), there are even "dual fuel" cooktops that offer both gas and electric-powered burners.

With any cooktop, look for easy-to-clean, hard-to-scratch surfaces, and make sure controls are intuitive to use. As with ranges, some of newer cooktop models include helpful indicator lights to alert you when a burner is on.

Wallovens Okay, take a deep breath: I'm about to commit culinary heresy. In wall-mounted styling, double ovens are *de rigueur*. But do you REALLY cook enough to warrant the additional cost and decreased storage/counter space of having two? Remember, too, that the original 1950s double ovens were a meager 24 inches wide. Today, they're a more commodious 27 or 30 inches. And thanks to superior insulating technology, the usable interior space has also grown. On the other hand, if you want to be able to roast a leg of lamb and bake a gently heated meringue at the same time, you don't have much choice: it's double ovens or dessert disaster!

TIPS FROM THE PROS:

"The biggest mistake that people make with wall ovens is to mount them at the wrong height. And with a double-oven arrangement, they're BOTH at the wrong height. Your oven's center rack should be situated at the point where your arms are the strongest, which is not when they're extended straight out, but rather when they're lowered slightly. Check it for yourself. Put something heavy in a roasting pan, and see what it's like to lift it at various heights. The optimum height will be slightly different for everybody."

—Rose Levy Beranbaum, author of The Cake Bible and The Pie & Pastry Bible

Hoods & ventilation

Picture a kitchen with no ventilation. Imagine the odors. The grease. The dirt. The condensation.

In an area as dynamic as the kitchen (think heat, water, smoke!), proper ventilation is obviously crucial.

There are two basic types of kitchen ventilating systems: The first, updraft, draws air upward and away from the cooking surface. Range hoods are the classic example of this updraft-style venting system. The second, downdraft, is typically located in or near the cooking surface itself and pulls air downward to filter it instead. Though downdraft systems tend to be slightly less effective than their updraft cousins (heat, after all, naturally rises), they are also less visually intrusive—perfect for island cooktops and other locations where an overhead hood would not be practical.

Both updraft- and downdraft-style ventilating systems may be either "ducted" or "duct-less." A ducted system is connected to a tube that vents stale, dirty air directly to the outside. A ductless system simply filters fumes and particles, but is less efficient at removing grease and will not remove condensation-producing moisture or gases such as carbon dioxide or carbon monoxide (which is why these systems are not recommended for use with gas ranges). Though the expense will be greater, if at all possible opt for a ducted ventilating system.

As with other kitchen appliances, features on range hoods and other ventilating systems are getting more technologically sophisticated all the time. Not only do many models now include push-button controls and built-in task lights, some now feature a slide-out glass visor for overhead units or, on down-draft models, a pop-up "snorkel" assembly—even indicator lights to let you know when it's time to change the filter.

Bells and whistles aside, be sure to consider both the fan's capacity AND its noise level before making your selection. Noise level will be rated in "sones"—the lower the number, the

I have a char-broiler in the house, which I really enjoy. I grill everything: vegetables, chickens, you name it! People tend to think about grilling only in the summer, but it's really nice in the winter, too.

—Ann Cooper, author and chef for The Putney Inn, Vermont

quieter the fan. But remember that fans are not the only source of ventilation noise; that roar you may hear in a highly ventilated kitchen could be air rushing through the duct, and not the fan at all. If you've got your heart set on having a kitchen that's library-quiet, consult an HVAC engineer to help you design the best possible solution. Venting capacity is rated in cubic feet per minute (or "cfm"). Again, your exact needs will depend on your particular cooking configuration. A fan that's rated at 350 cfm may be more than adequate for kitchens with standard appliances, while those boasting commercial-style ranges may require one that's rated at 1,200 cfm.

Check with your range or cooktop manufacturer for any venting specifications or recommendations, and with the vent manufacturer for recommended mounting distances from the cooking surface, etc. For more complex ventilating questions, you may also want to consult an air-quality specialist; check your Yellow Pages under "Air Quality—Indoor." Local building codes should also be consulted, particularly if you plan to install a commercial or oversize range.

Some rough rules of thumb: For wall- or ceiling-mounted exhaust fans, the Home Ventilating Institute recommends a ventilation system that will produce 15 air changes per hour and offers this helpful hint: assuming your kitchen has a standard 8-foot ceiling, you can determine the necessary CFM to produce that amount of air movement by multiplying your kitchen's floor area by 2. For kitchen range hood fans, HVI recommends a minimum of 40 CFM per lineal foot of range hood and adds that "higher ratings than minimums are often desirable."

But remember that a larger exhaust fan, by itself, is not necessarily better. Using an oversize fan can actually waste energy by removing excessive amounts of expensively air-conditioned or heated indoor air. And an oversize system may also force you to supplement room air with an additional source for outside air (called a "makeup air duct") to prevent the flow of combustion gases back into your house.

TIPS FROM THE PROS:

"Proper venting is one of the most important considerations in a kitchen. Many of the range hoods shown in the magazines are the same size as the cooktop. For maximum collection of that grease-laden smoke, it's far better if they're six inches wider than the cooktop. And the fan motor should be mounted on the roof, if possible, for quietness."

—Rose Levy Beranbaum, author of *The Cake Bible* and *The Pie & Pastry Bible*

TIPS FROM THE PROS:

"When you choose a range or stovetop, take a look at where the knobs are located. On my stovetop, the knobs are up on top near the burners—and every time I cook they get dirty. It's a question of practicality—how much do you want to clean? If possible, try to limit the number of places that dirt, oil, and grease can collect. There may be other considerations for some folks, of course. If you have small children, for example, it may not be best to have controls located down on the side where small fingers can reach."

—Lisa Schroeder, Owner, Mother's Bistro & Bar

The majority of wall-ovens are electric, but within that basic category is a growing range of options. Choose from traditional thermal designs, or the increasingly popular convection models. Or opt for a hybridized thermal-convection—or even a thermal-convection-microwave—style.

As you review features, be sure to compare actual interior dimensions. Differing designs and insulating materials may translate into more or less usable baking space in similar-size models.

For those with money to burn—or at least steam gently—there's even a new twist on ovens: the warming drawer. If you've so much as glanced at an interior-design magazine lately, you'll have seen pictures of these hot-on-the-kitchen-scene innovations. Temperature- and moisture-controlled, these specialized under-counter compartments are designed to keep casseroles and other dishes warm prior to serving. Here again, weigh your actual culinary needs against your wish list.

"I have a big, old Garland gas stove at my home in Boston which I've had for years, and I just love it. I'm also used to working on an electric stovetop on my television show, so I find that either gas or electric works so long as it's powerful—you want to have very high heat when you need it. Many of the gas stoves made for home use don't get hot enough. If so, I think you're better off with a good electric."

—Julia Child, author of *The French Chef Cookbook*

convection

What's all the hoopla about the new "convection" ovens?

The principle of convection cooking is actually pretty simple: a fan circulates the heated air inside the oven to eliminate cold spots and ensure even cooking. More basic designs simply add a fan that circulates the heat from the usual elements built into the top and bottom of the oven. Higher-end convection ovens are designed with an additional heating element in the back of the oven, protected by a baffle.

The really great news about convection cooking, though, is in the bottom line; the proof, as they say, is in the pudding! Because temperatures in a convection oven remain uniform, food cooks more evenly and baking times can be reduced by as much as 25 or 30 percent. (At least one new design that uses jets of hot air aimed directly at food claims to reduce cooking times by as much as 75 percent.) And that means important savings, not just in time but also in energy bills!

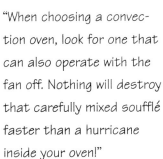

TIPS FROM THE PROS:

"When choosing a convection oven, look for one that can also operate with the fan off. Nothing will destroy that carefully mixed soufflé faster than a hurricane inside your oven!"

—Michael Pantano, FCSI, commercial kitchen planner

Microwaves

A microwave's a microwave—right? Well, yes and no. When it comes to microwave cooking, size counts. Size of its wattage, that is. The higher the watts, the faster the cooking time.

Before you decide on such features as a turntable, consider: What are the dimensions (and limitations) of the space where your microwave will be mounted? Will it sit on your countertop, mount under the cabinet, or a built-in exhaust fan for positioning over a gas stovetop? How large an interior capacity do you need for the dishes you typically use? Would one larger microwave be the answer to your kitchen prayers? Or would you really be better off with one large and one small—or perhaps two smaller—models?

The virtues of a turntable-model are considerable (no constant reaching in to shift contents), and they're no longer that expensive. Other options you may want to consider include a turntable on/off function (to accommodate larger platters), or perhaps a combination microwave-convection oven, which allows you to brown or roast.

Refrigerators

Give your tape measure an extra workout before heading out to buy a new refrigerator. Not only will you need to measure the size of your cabinet opening, but you should pay special attention to door and drawer clearances as well. A side-by-side refrigerator, for example, may call for extra width to allow doors—and therefore drawers—to open fully.

Don't forget to measure distances to nearby doors, counters, and other obstacles while you're at it. I've seen refrigerators tucked neatly in their designated slot—with doors that

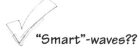

"Smart"-waves??

Never quite mastered all those buttons, settings, and programs on your microwave? You may be in luck. Microwaves themselves are getting smarter. Tests are already planned for a microwave that can scan the bar code on a convenience food and figure out for itself exactly how long and at what temperature to cook the product. And it can even flash an ingredients warning if you're allergic to peanuts or other common food items.

miss a center island by mere millimeters when you swing them open. (Not a pretty sight for traffic flow, either; just try to sidle by when someone is reaching for the milk carton!)

While there's an understandable tendency to go for the biggest model that will fit your space, some avid cooks who shop for fresh produce nearly every day find they don't really NEED a gargantuan refrigerator. And remember that size has its trade-offs: a smaller refrigerator may allow you more valuable countertop room.

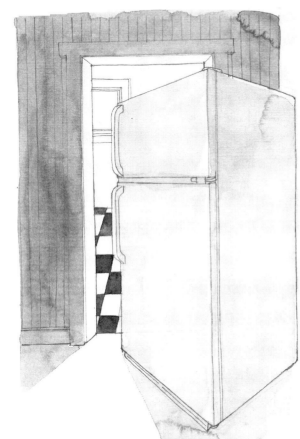

Configuration? Well, that's largely a matter of personal preference, of course. Most of us find the conventional freezer-on-the-top style useful and reasonably convenient. Or at least we're used to it. But give at least a passing thought to alternate arrangements. I was tickled pink when I saw my first refrigerator with the freezer on the bottom—it just made so much sense. That "upside-down" configuration permits most-frequently-used refrigerated items to be kept at eye level and takes advantage of the principle that cold air naturally sinks. Since these models are less popular, however, you'll find fewer styles and options available.

Yet another option is the side-by-side style refrigerator. Since doors are narrower, less "swing-room" clearance is required in front. And there's space for both frozen and refrigerated foods in the center "comfort zone" area. There is a price to pay for side-by-side convenience, however: shelves are typically narrower and shallower than in traditional styles. And the price tag on side-by-side models tends to run a bit higher as well. But, of course, shallower shelves do have one advantage: That container of leftover spaghetti is less likely to be overlooked.

Measure access clearances
before you shop.

Not so very long ago, there was no such thing as a "built-in" refrigerator in residential kitchens; freestanding models were your only choice. Today in luxe kitchens you may have to blink twice to figure out which

What's Cool On The Cold Front?

TIP:

Getting rid of an old refrigerator? Call your electric company to see whether they offer a rebate program if you purchase a more energy-efficient model.

They haven't yet designed a refrigerator that will mix your favorite martini or pop that frozen dinner into the microwave for you. But it seems they've come up with just about everything else.

Newer options include shelves that adjust with a simple turn of a handle; built-in water filtration systems for ice-making and water-on-the door models; a through-the-door niche for quick access to frequently used items; and custom "trim kits" that allow you to dress your refrigerator in a wide range of colors.

There's also a rapidly expanding selection of specialized ("modular") units on the market today: a beverage chiller with built-in wine racks, and a cabinet-mounted refrigerated drawer for fresh vegetables and baking goods, for example. Sure, such "extras" can be pricey. The advantage? Convenience. And for some folks, the best refrigeration solution may be to make use of two smaller units—for example, a modest conventional refrigerator plus a refrigerated drawer near the primary work area for fresh produce or baking needs.

"cabinet" actually hides the ice cream. Built-in model refrigerators are designed to fit flush with cabinets and are finished with a cabinet-style front to blend in. The downsides: They're also shallower, to match cabinet depth, and (you guessed it) a bit more expensive than freestanding models.

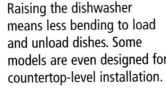

Raising the dishwasher means less bending to load and unload dishes. Some models are even designed for countertop-level installation.

Dishwashers

Thanks in part to new energy standards that went into effect in 1994, today's dishwashers are more efficient than ever before. They also offer more features—and quieter operation.

Here, too, models run the features gamut: folding tines for greater loading flexibility, grinders to make short work of food scraps, special racks for utensils, "top-rack-only" washing options, and so forth. And of course you'll find reversible color panels, stylish recessed handles, and touch-pad controls.

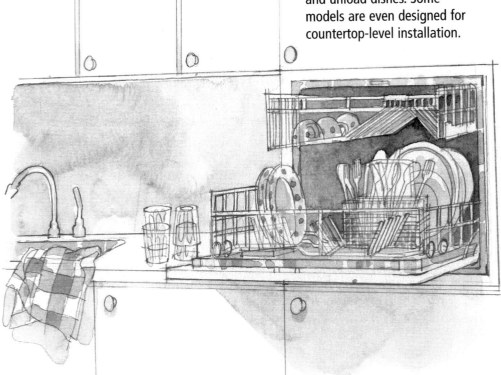

Beyond the purely aesthetic, however, you'll want to pay attention to how the unit is constructed. Some top-of-the-line models feature stainless-steel interior to prevent rust and chips and maximize heat retention, for example. How about the unit's filtering system? Is there a removable trap that you'll need to clean manually, or does the unit take care of scrap disposal automatically?

TIPS FROM THE PROS:

"Some compactors require you to use special, proprietary garbage bags—a never-ending expense, particularly when compared to using those designer kraft-paper-brown freebies that the grocery story hands out with every purchase ... assuming, of course, you correctly answer that grocery goodbye mantra— "Plastic or paper?""

—Michael Pantano, FCSI, commercial kitchen planner

Ask about "energy saver" options as well. Some models offer a programmable "delayed start" setting so you can time your use to take advantage of off-peak utility rates, for example.

As anyone who's ever tried to carry on a phone conversation with a dishwasher running knows, these domestic monsters can be—well, monstrously noisy. More expensive models feature both quieter pumps and motors and more noise-dampening insulation.

One recent trend in dishwasher installation is to locate the unit higher than floor level; the NKBA now recommends installing dishwashers 9 to 12 inches off the floor. The advantage, of course, is that loading and unloading is easier on your back. BUT remember that you'll lose the counter work area that's usually available over a traditional in-cabinet installation.

Just as refrigerator manufacturers have come out with special mini drawer-size models, dishwashing designers are also having a field day with "drawer"-style technology. Though capacity is limited (about a dozen dinner plates), each load also requires significantly less water than a full-size model. And aficionados note that you may never need to unload and stack dishes again; simply install two, and use tableware straight from the "clean" drawer while you load up the other.

Trash Compactor

Yet another of those "personal" choices: the trash compactor. People either love 'em or they—well, don't see much reason to bother.

On the plus side, a trash compactor can compress a dozen or more average-size garbage bags into a single (as the name implies) *compact* unit. The downside: that one remaining bag will weigh the same as the 12 to 14 trash bags you've stuffed into that single bundle.

If you decide a trash compactor will make your kitchen chores easier—or at least reduce the number of times you have to yell at someone to take the trash out—look for a design that permits bag removal with a minimum of lifting, and allows for easy cleanup.

Lighting Options

Not to point fingers at either gender, but when I first roamed from counter to counter and found my shadow over every workspace in my kitchen, I *knew* it wasn't designed by someone who does a lot of cooking!

If you've ever had to squint at a recipe or been blinded by a harsh fluorescent's glare, you know how important proper lighting is to a comfortable, workable kitchen. But before you simply stick up another light fixture or two, take the time to *really* evaluate your kitchen lighting needs.

In general, kitchen lighting goals are three-fold: glare-free general illumination; adequate workspace or "task" lighting (with no shadows, please!); and "accent" lighting to create or enhance a mood.

We'll talk about each of these in more detail below. But before we do, here are a few questions you'll need to weigh about your particular kitchen:

✎ Where—and how large—are the windows?

✎ Which way do they face? What times of day do you get good, natural light?

✎ What colors are your walls and cabinets? (Dark woods? White paint? Reflective finishes?)

✎ How high is your ceiling?

✎ Are there kitchen features you would like to accent—or hide?

✎ Where do you need more light—or less glare—on work areas?

✎ What sort of mood would you like lighting to help create?

Your answers may point you in some pretty clear directions. You'll obviously need more artificial light in a deep-burgundy room with a North-facing window, for example, than in an all-white kitchen with a huge West-facing bay. Mood-enhancing choices, on the other hand, may require a bit more pondering.

Give yourself time to really think about what you need and want your lighting to do for you. Pay attention to what works—and what doesn't—in your friends' kitchens. Browse a lighting store for some eye-opening options. There is a huge variety of lighting products on the market, with fixtures to fit just about every need and budget. In many situations, the best lighting solutions are ones that provide some measure of adjustment. Whenever possible, look for fixtures than can be raised or lowered, or dimmer-controlled.

No ONE lighting solution will meet all of your needs, of course. As we've mentioned above, most experts break lighting down into three distinct varieties:

Ambient or *general* lighting provides a soft, well-diffused light throughout the room. While the classic ambient light-provider is a ceiling fixture, we're a long way from that one lonely bulb in the center of the room that my grandmother knew! Upward-directed track lights or an illuminated soffit around the room's perimeter can also provide good ambient lighting, particularly when designed to allow light to reflect off the ceiling. And at least in the daytime, natural window light is an excellent—and free—source of ambient light.

Whatever style or combination of ambient lights you choose, consider adding a dimmer switch to expand your lighting choices. (Note: Dimmers are not an option for many types of fluorescent fixtures, however. See below.)

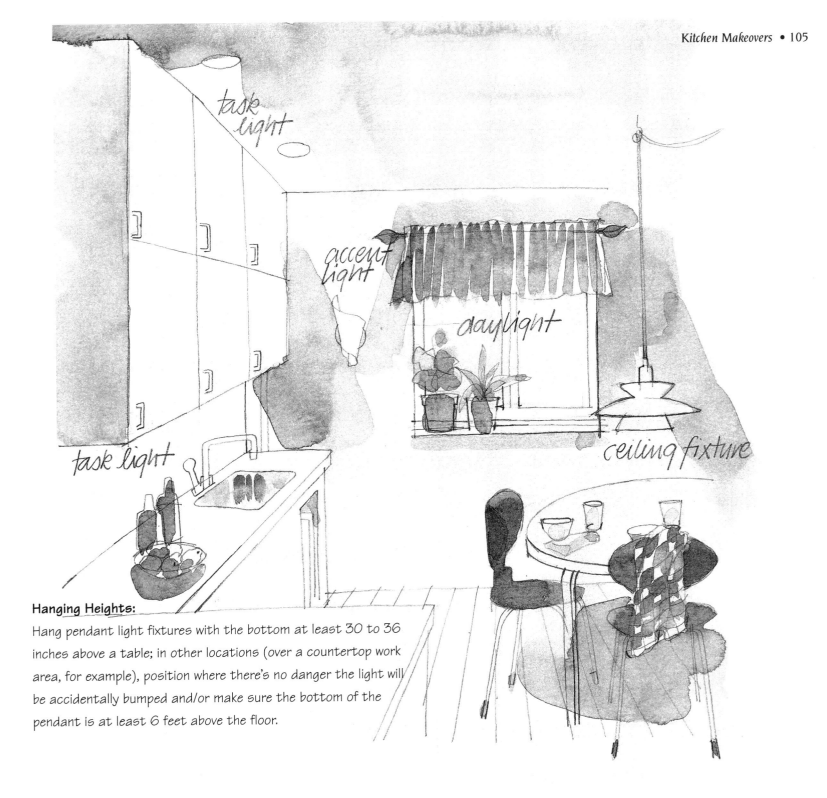

task light

accent light

daylight

task light

ceiling fixture

Hanging Heights:

Hang pendant light fixtures with the bottom at least 30 to 36 inches above a table; in other locations (over a countertop work area, for example), position where there's no danger the light will be accidentally bumped and/or make sure the bottom of the pendant is at least 6 feet above the floor.

In addition to general room lighting, it's important to plan for *task lighting* at high-utilization work areas such as the sink, range or cooktop, chopping block, baking station, or other food preparation zone, and desk or menu-planning area. Task lighting is often accomplished using highly focused light styles: Recessed can lights, single-bulb spots or even track lights are popular choices in this genre. And I love the look of some of the exotic new droplights, also known as pendants—just make sure they won't hit your head or otherwise get in your way (some adjust in height as needed).

When it comes to task lighting, design folks have apparently become increasingly aware of the need for good under-cabinet lighting, as the range of options in that subspecialty has exploded in recent years. (My kitchen is obviously not alone in the shadow department!) Because under-cabinet lighting tends to be close to eye level, make sure you choose a style that's adequately shielded to prevent glare.

Though usually you want task lighting to be bright and relatively focused, here again, a dimmer switch can help make lighting more versatile. Consider using a dimmer on task-lighting circuits to give you a night light or mood-setting option when the kitchen is not in "work mode."

If task lighting is the workhorse in the kitchen lighting scene, *accent lighting* is the playful child. Add drama or panache with lighted wall sconces. Highlight an interesting architectural feature, a wondrous work of art, or a frivolous frill by adding its very own spotlight. Adorn shelf edges and nooks with strip lights. Even festoon your favorite plants with glittering miniature lights! Accent lighting is a relatively inexpensive way to let your imagination run wild.

Code Considerations:

Replacing an existing light fixture with a newer one is usually a pretty simple operation. But what if you don't already have a fixture in the right place? And what if your wish list includes several new lights?

If all you're adding is one new fixture, your contractor will probably be able to simply extend an existing light circuit and "fish" the wires to a new location. But if your plan involves three new sconces, two fluorescent panels and six recessed can lights, you may need to have a professional electrician add another circuit—or two—from your electrical panel to handle the load. All electrical work, of course, must be done to code and you'll need a permit if you'll be running any new wires or adding circuits. Recessed can lights and halogen lights in particular can be a fire hazard if they're not installed properly. Unless you're absolutely sure of what you're doing, call a licensed contractor for help getting your new lights on-line!

Turn Off That Switch—and Switch That Bulb!

Your mother was right. Flipping the lights off—or at least changing the KIND of bulb you burn—can make a difference!

Lighting accounts for 20 to 25 percent of all electricity consumed in the United States. Not all of that is residential lighting, of course. But the more than 3 billion light fixtures in American homes today draw about 138 billion kilowatt-hours of energy per year to operate—and cost consumers nearly $11 billion annually. As much as half of residential lighting energy in a typical home is wasted by obsolete equipment or inefficient use.

The good news: replacing just one-quarter of traditional incandescent bulbs (those in "high use" sockets such as your kitchen, living room, and outdoor fixtures) with energy-efficient alternatives could cut national lighting energy usage by a whopping 70 billion kilowatt-hours a year—more than half!

—Sources: publications issued by the EPA's Energy Star Program and DOE's National Renewable Energy Laboratory.

TIP:

Planning to add an array of fluorescent fixtures on top of your cabinets, concealed by a valance? To permit maximum light to shine into the room, edge the fixture forward (away from the wall) and angle the top of the valance slightly toward the room.

Fluorescent vs. Incandescent vs. Halogen

As you shop for lighting fixtures, you'll be bombarded with choices, choices, choices! While styles (and, of course, prices!) vary widely, here's the lowdown on the three most popular lighting types:

✔ **Incandescent** is the type of light produced by those ubiquitous rounded bulbs you probably grew up with. The warm, friendly light from these inexpensive bulbs is produced from resistance as electric current travels through the bulb's filament (usually tungsten). The downside of incandescent lights is that they're normally not high on the energy-efficiency scale; incandescent bulbs may waste as much as 90 percent of the energy that flows through them as heat! On the other hand, incandescent lights (unlike many fluorescents) have one important virtue: they can be controlled with a dimmer, allowing you to vary the intensity of the light as needed.

✔ **Fluorescent** fixtures produce light by exciting the atoms inside a gas-filled tube. Though fluorescent bulbs are more expensive up front than regular incandescent bulbs, they're cost-savers in the long run because fluorescents are significantly more energy-efficient and long-lasting. How much more? Fluorescents can produce the same amount of light using only one-quarter to one-fifth the wattage as incandescent bulbs, and can last up to twenty times as long! That helps to explain why in some parts of the country a fluorescent kitchen fixture is now required in new-home construction.

While older fluorescents were prone to flickering and tended to yield a cold, artificial-looking light, newer bulb technology has overcome both of these drawbacks.

Fluorescent bulbs now offer both warm- and cool-light styles; some even duplicate the spectrum of natural daylight. BUT because most ballasts are not designed for a variable power source, the majority of fluorescent fixtures cannot be dimmer-controlled.

One notable new development: compact fluorescent lights (CFLs). These offer the extended life and high-efficiency of larger fluorescent fixtures in (as the name implies) a more compact, bulb-like form. And unlike many of their larger cousins, some CFLs can even be operated on a dimmer.

✔ **Halogen**, a relative newcomer to the lighting scene, uses halogen gas inside the tube to produce a bright, intense light in a compact package. Three times as bright and twice as long-lasting as incandescents, halogen bulbs are typically (though not always) designed as low-voltage systems (requiring use of a transformer to step down standard household current—a slight additional expense). But because halogen bulbs get extremely hot, it's important to mount them exactly according to manufacturers' instructions to avoid fire danger, and place where you won't accidentally brush against a hot lens. Use sparingly in climates where the generated heat is a consideration.

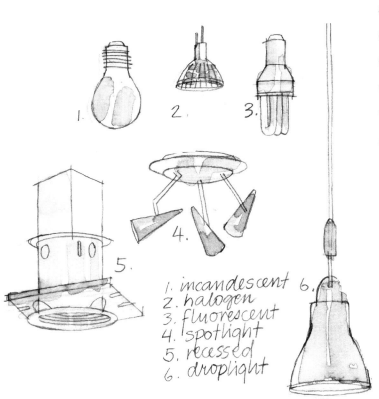

1. incandescent
2. halogen
3. fluorescent
4. spotlight
5. recessed
6. droplight

Lighting Layout

✔ To prevent shadows on a countertop work area, position overhead lights to shine directly downward; for best illumination with multiple lights, space so their patterns will overlap slightly.

✔ For countertop lighting that must come from behind, angle the light from a direction opposite your dominant hand (for right-handed people, direct the light over the left shoulder; for left-handed folks, over the right shoulder).

Windows

Adding or enlarging windows is a wonderful way to improve the ambient light in a kitchen. And especially if you're replacing older, less energy-efficient windows, over time it can also be a major energy saver!

What *style* of window (double-hung; casement; slider) you choose is largely a matter of aesthetics and personal preference. If you're remodeling an older home, for example, you may want to choose windows that closely resemble the originals to maintain the architectural "look and feel" of the building. But remember that energy efficiency should be considered, too! Tight-sealing casements, for example, tend to be more energy-saving than sliders or double-hung designs.

Just how complicated a window project will be depends in part on whether or not you will be able to make use of the existing framing inside your wall. If you're simply swapping the existing window for another of identical size, chances are the job should be fairly quick and easy. If, however, you're planning to enlarge an existing opening—or perhaps create a window where none presently exists—you're biting off a bit more work.

Some manufacturers now make sash-replacement kits that allow you to replace only the sash units without changing the outside frame, a potential time-saver and a way to preserve more of the original construction in a vintage house. But experienced builders caution that installing even replacement kits can pose difficulties if the existing frames are crooked or turn out to need repair.

Take a look at the illustration on page 123—that's what the inside of your walls would look like if you removed the surface layer of drywall or plaster. Structurally, it's not really very complicated. The studs carry the weight of the roof and also provide a place to attach the exterior siding and interior wall materials. The spaces between the studs are

TIPS FROM THE PROS:

"Adding or enlarging a window may have positive side effects well beyond simply improving the visual attributes of the room. According to Feng Shui, the ancient Chinese art of placement, good natural lighting and the circulation of fresh air can help to activate the chi, or vital energy, of the residents in the house."

—Helen Jay, author of *Paper Dragons: Journey to the Shamanic Roots of Feng Shui* and co-director of the Feng Shui Designs Learning Center in Nevada City, California

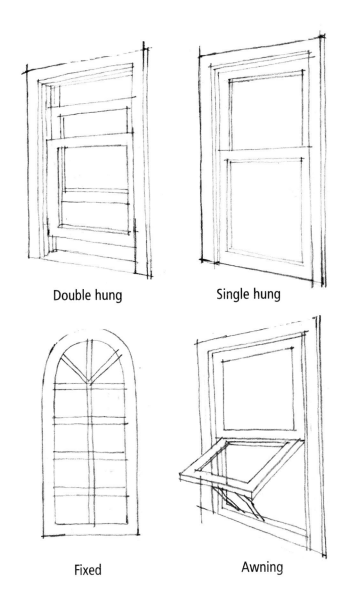

Double hung

Single hung

Fixed

Awning

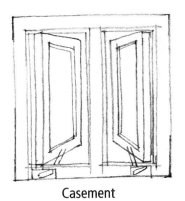

Casement

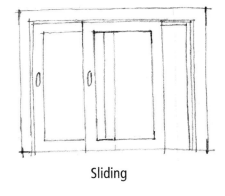

Sliding

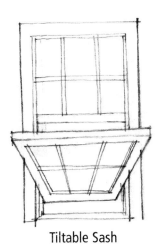

Tiltable Sash

usually filled with insulation of one sort or another, and may have plumbing and electrical runs through them as well.

If you are going to cut a series of studs to make an opening for a window, you'll have to add what's known as a "header" to carry the load (downward force) that you're interrupting. The bigger the opening, the beefier the header that's required. Your contractor or local building department can help you choose the correct size for your particular window project (and because it's a structural matter, don't forget you'll also need to obtain a permit!)

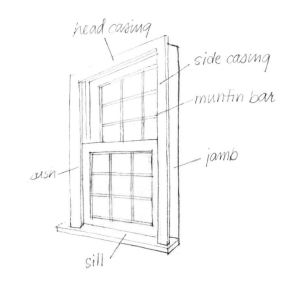

New windows usually come as a unit, and they may mount in several different ways. Follow your manufacturer's installation instructions carefully. In general, you'll set your new window into the framed opening, use a level to make sure it's square and level, then nail or screw the window in place through the jambs or a special mounting flange. Trim pieces are nailed in place to finish off the installation on the outside, and molding is generally used to complete the look on the inside. Depending on how much demolition was required to frame the new opening, you may also need to patch interior drywall or plaster.

Window Shopping

If you grew up in a cold, drafty house as I did, you don't need an engineer to tell you that glass makes a lousy insulator. According to the U.S. Department of Energy, the cost to offset unwanted heat losses and gains through residential and commercial windows totaled a whopping $20 billion in 1990 alone—one-fourth of all space heating and cooling energy!

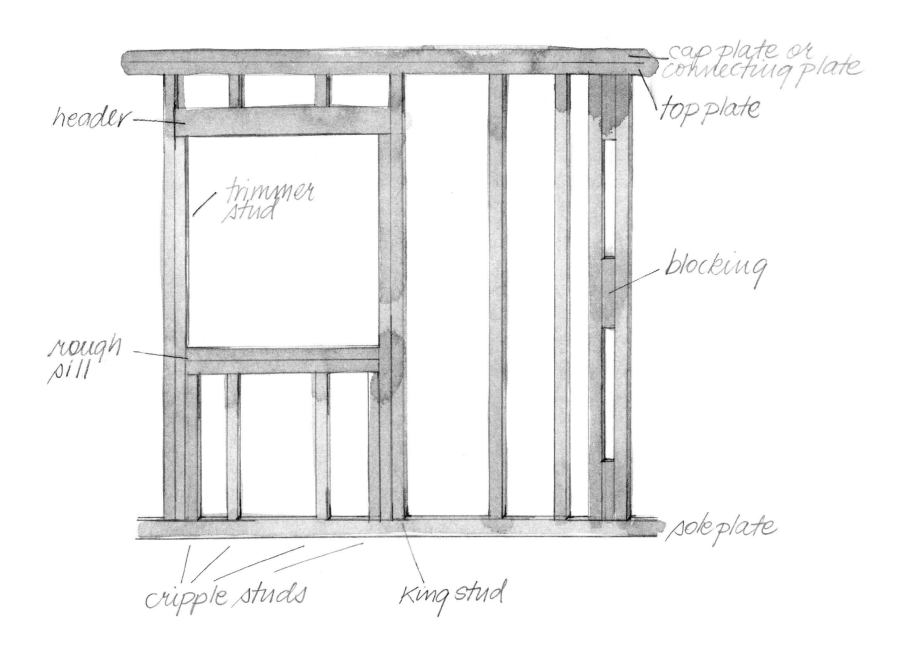

header

trimmer stud

rough sill

cripple studs

king stud

cap plate or connecting plate

top plate

blocking

sole plate

What does that mean to *your* wallet? Heating and cooling costs make up about 44 percent of a typical residential utility bill. The heat that exits through your windows can account for 10 to 25 percent of your winter heating bill, while heat gain through windows can inflate your summer cooling costs by up to 40 percent. Don't expect replacing windows alone to work miracles, however. Even installing new windows that are *twice* as energy-efficient as the old ones may cut your utility bills by only 6 to 10 percent. But remember, that's 6 to 10 percent *every month*. And that can add up!

Luckily, a number of design advances in the last decade have significantly improved the thermal performance of windows. Somewhat less fortunately for consumers, the new technology has also generated a confusing slew of new terms and acronyms. We'll talk about R-values, U-values, low-e coatings, SHGC ratings and air infiltration below. Depending upon where you live, some of these energy factors may be more important to you than others.

If you have single-pane windows (and nearly half of U.S. homes still do), replacing all of them with Energy Star (R) windows could slash up to 15 percent off your heating and cooling bills!

Source: U.S. Department of Energy's "Energy Star" program

Back to luckily again: Beginning in 1998, the DOE/EPA and the window industry have helped to take some of the confusion out of choosing an energy-efficient window for your particular location. Windows with the "Energy Star" label are *twice* as efficient as the average window produced just a decade ago and are 40 percent more energy-efficient than products required under the most common national building codes. And to help consumers make wise choices for their particular location, these windows' performance criteria are flagged as appropriate for northern, central, or southern regions using an easy-to-read, color-coded map.

Let's take a closer look at some of the energy buzzwords you'll encounter when you go window-shopping:

R-Value and U-Value: R-Value refers to a window's *resistance* to heat transfer—so a high number is better. U-Value measures the opposite—heat transfer or how much heat will escape through the window, so the lower the value the better. Some manufacturers give values for both the entire window and at the center-of-glass; the number for the entire window will give you a better indicator of its overall performance. (For those who are mathematically inclined, you can convert R-Value to U-Value by dividing 1 by the R-Value, and vice versa.)

Because they evaluate a window's susceptibility to heat loss, these figures will be particularly important for folks who live in colder climates. Factors that affect a window's R-Value (and therefore also its U-Value) include:

✔ The kind of glazing material used (glass, plastic)

✔ The number of glazing layers (single-, double-, or triple-pane)

✔ The size of the gaps between layers

✔ Whether an insulating coating or gas (argon or krypton) has been used between the glass layers

✔ The frame's material and design

To give you a rough idea, an energy-inefficient single-glazed window might have an R-Value of 0.9 and a U-Value of about 1.1. A window with reasonably good energy efficiency may have an R-Value of 2.5 and a U-Value of approximately .40. And a top-of-the-line window designed for extremely cold climates might have an R-Value of 6.7 and a U-Value of about .15. When comparing the R- or U-values of various window manufacturers, make certain you're evaluating windows of the same size and style, and that both refer to the entire window unit and not simply the center-of-glass.

Low-e Coatings: Low-e coatings are just one of the ways manufacturers have been able to make windows more energy-efficient. Originally designed for use in colder cli-

Windows Of The Future: "Smart windows" may eventually help conserve even more energy dollars. In the works: special "chromogenic" glazings that will automatically change their heat- and light-transmission characteristics in response to changes in temperature and sunlight. Consumers may also have more information available to help them choose windows in the future. The National Fenestration Rating Council, a nonprofit, public/private organization that currently operates several programs to rate and label windows, is working on developing additional ratings for air infiltration, condensation resistance, long-term energy performance, seasonal heating and cooling, and optical properties.

mates, "low-e" stands for low emissivity—meaning it reduces the transfer (emission) of heat. The high-tech trick? A microscopic metal coating that's applied to one side of the glass, typically facing the air space between panes. While light still passes through very successfully, the coating reflects 40 to 70 percent of any heat that's trying to escape back inside your home. And low-e coatings may even reduce furniture-fading UV rays by up to 75 percent. (Remember, however, that some houseplants need UV to thrive!)

Now, engineers have figured out that various sorts of coatings can also be beneficial in Southern climates, as well. Special "spectrally selective" low-e coatings, "heat absorbing" glazing and "heat reflective" coatings can help stop heat GAIN in parts of the country where air conditioning is a significant energy expense. And that takes us to our next acronym.

Solar Heat Gain Coefficient (SHGC): Solar Heat Gain Coefficient, or SHGC, measures the shading properties of a window—a factor that's particularly important for warm climates.

As you would expect, the more darkly tinted the glass, the better it will shade the interior of your home from transfer of solar heat. Gray- and bronze-tinted windows are the most common, but blue- and green-tinted windows are also available. More tinting is not always better, of course; houseplants may suffer when windows transmit less than 70 percent of visible light, and totally black window coatings are discouraged in hot climates because they absorb (and re-radiate) considerable heat, while making extra electric lights necessary!

Special "heat-absorbing" or "reflective" coatings are sometimes used with tinted glass to reduce the transmission of heat. And a window's shading properties can also be improved through new "spectrally selective" low-e coatings, which can filter out between 40 to 70 percent of the heat normally passing through clear glass, while permitting the full amount of visible light to reach the inside.

SHGC numbers range in decimal increments from zero (totally blocked) to one (the equivalent of an untinted single pane of glass). To help reduce cooling costs, look for lower SHGC numbers; the lower the number, the better the window will protect against

TIP:

If cost is a factor, consider replacing windows in the poorest condition and/or on the most energy-sensitive side of your house first. In cold climates, target north-facing windows; in hotter climes, start with south- or west-facing windows.

solar heat transfer to the inside. You might find dark-tinted glass with an SHGC of .15, for example, while less protective and almost clear glass would be .85. To qualify for the Energy Star (R) label for Southern climates, windows, doors and skylights must have a SHGC rating of 0.40 or below.

Air Infiltration: The energy efficiency of a window is also affected by the amount of air leakage or "infiltration" it allows—a number that's usually expressed in terms of cubic feet per minute, per square foot of window area. A fairly tight window might have an air infiltration rating of .1 or .2, for example, while a rather loose-fitting window might be .5. The style of window will also affect how much air infiltration it permits. Casement windows (the kind that crank open) tend to be tighter than double-hung windows or sliders, for example. Most experts suggest you look for windows with air infiltration ratings of 0.2 or less.

TIPS FROM THE PROS:

"When choosing a high-quality window, I advise people to look for a factory warrantee of 20 years or more against seal failure, 15 years or better on hardware, and at least 1 to 2 years on parts and labor. And because the warrantee is only as good as the company that stands behind it, a company with many years in business is usually a safer choice than one that has not been around a long time. "But just as important as choosing a quality window manufacturer is choosing a quality installer; I've seen a surprising number of window failures caused by poor installation. Newer windows are a complex, sealed system. If the installer applies too much pressure trying to force the frames or sash into place, it can stress the seals and result in premature failure. Check out the company by asking for a list of 10 not-so-recent customers. Then ask those clients if they had a problem within 1 to 2 years of the date their windows were installed, and how willing the company was to fix the problem."

—Michael Lamb, Energy Efficiency & Renewable Energy Clearinghouse

A Look At Frames

When you're choosing windows, you'll also have to choose among a multitude of window frame materials.

Wood, the long-term favorite, is considered by many to be the most attractive alternative. Wood offers excellent insulating qualities (according to the Wood Products Promotion Council, it's more than 1,770 times more thermal resistant than aluminum.) But wood-framed windows will require periodic painting to stay beautiful. And wood frames are generally pricier than either vinyl or aluminum.

One hybrid worth noting: some windows are now vinyl- or aluminum-clad on the outside for a virtually maintenance-free exterior, while preserving the beauty of natural wood on the interior face.

Vinyl-framed windows, by contrast, are extremely low-maintenance and may cost only about half what wood windows do. Typically constructed of polyvinyl chloride (PVC), vinyl frames first made their appearance in the 1970s, and offer good insulating properties in addition to a range of never-paint color options. Because it's not quite as strong as some other frame materials, larger sizes of vinyl-framed windows may contain steel or aluminum reinforcing.

TIPS FROM THE PROS:

"Vinyl-framed windows may be either heat-welded or screwed together at the joints. Some manufacturers like to tout their heat-welded corners, but it's really a development to help the factory save money on screws and labor. Either method will work just fine; neither is really stronger or superior in any way that's important to the consumer. If heat welding is not done carefully, it can distort the weatherstripping groove and cause energy-wasting gaps at the corners. So it's a good idea to inspect the condition of the weatherstripping at the corners of heat-welded windows before the window is installed.

"One more tip: If you plan to install vinyl windows on south-facing exposures, look for windows that contain a high-quality UV-inhibitor to help prevent sun damage like small cracks and brittleness."

—*Michael Lamb, EREC*

TIPS

✔ Well-crafted windows will have quality hardware and quality materials. Remember that the cheapest windows may not be the bargain they appear to be. Over time, inexpensively made windows may crack, develop condensation between the panes, and frames may warp or corrode.

✔ Window dimensions are always expressed with the HORIZONTAL measurement first, THEN the vertical. A 2-0 x 6-0 window, in other words, will be tall and skinny; if that's what you want, be careful you don't order a 6-0 x 2-0 window by mistake!

✔ Windows can be custom-made to fit virtually any opening. But you'll save a considerable amount of money if you size your openings to accommodate standard (stock) window sizes.

When specifying a window size, the horizontal measurement is written first.

Newer frame options include fiberglass, composite plastics, and polyester resin. These tough man-made materials offer a range of colors along with the advantages of low maintenance, and excellent R-values. One notable advantage to fiberglass is that its expansion and contraction rates closely mimic that of ordinary window glass, so the fit is more likely to stay airtight.

Often least expensive of all are aluminum window frames. Though low-maintenance and durable, aluminum frames tend to conduct heat more easily than other materials. To minimize the thermal disadvantages, look for a frame designed with a "thermal break" (a strip of rubber or plastic) between the interior and exterior of the frame to limit conductivity. Aluminum windows may be fine for moderate regions and stand up well in areas of high wind. But they generally aren't the best choice for climates with temperature extremes.

Garden windows

One variation on the window theme is a three-dimensional window unit. Popularly known as "box bays" (if they have straight sides), "angled bays" (with angled sides), or "sun" bays (if they have a glass roof), they're updated versions of what used to be called a garden or greenhouse window.

Whatever style you prefer, garden windows are a terrific way to expand and brighten a small or even a not-so-small kitchen. And they can be a great place to grow and display herbs and other small plants. As with other windows, you'll want to pay attention to R-values as you make your selection. And if you live in a hot climate and/or plan to use the garden window to grow plants, you'll also want to give extra thought to solar heat-gain concerns and ventilating options to make sure your window won't bake the begonias—or heat up your house!

The exact technique for installing each garden window will depend on the window's design, the type of exterior siding on your home, and whether or not the garden window is replacing another window of similar size. Larger garden windows (those wider than about 5 feet) may require special mounting brackets or cables to help support their weight. Read and follow your manufacturer's installation instructions carefully.

Skylights

A skylight can be a dramatic way to lighten and brighten a dreary kitchen space, particularly when adding other types of windows isn't an option. And skylight styles that can be opened bring in not only light but also fresh air!

Though not overwhelmingly complex, installing a skylight does require familiarity with both tools and basic construction techniques. For all but the very smallest skylights, you'll need to cut at least one roof rafter and frame in a new opening to transfer the roof loads and support the skylight unit. While newer designs have made significant improvements over some of the older, leak-prone models, you'll still need to be extra careful to create a perfectly waterproof seal around the opening. Typically, this is accomplished using some combination of metal flashing, caulking, roof cement, and carefully merging these new materials with the existing roof tiles or shingles. Unless you're working with either a flat roof (often not a good candidate for a skylight!) or a cathedral ceiling, you'll also need to construct a "light well" to conduct the light between the roof and interior ceiling.

One recently introduced alternative to a traditional skylight: a light TUBE. These tubes use a highly reflective tubing material in place of the traditional drywall light shaft to transmit ambient light into the space below. Since less light is lost in transit, light tubes can deliver significantly more light than a similar-size skylight. Some models claim

TIPS FROM THE PROS:

"Skylights can be beautiful but there is a downside: they're notoriously energy inefficient. I made that mistake myself—and I've regretted it for the last 15 years! Remember that skylights represent holes in your thermal envelope, and the best skylights are rated only about R-4 or R-6, compared to R-38 for the attic insulation they are making a hole in. To minimize unwanted summer heat gain and winter heat loss, keep any skylights small, and use them only in mild climates."

—Michael Lamb

to deliver up to 95 percent of the light they collect, while absorbing 99 percent of harmful UV rays. Perhaps best of all, many of these compact units are designed to fit between existing roof rafters, so they're easier to install than conventional skylights—no structural retrofitting required. And they're considerably less expensive, too: as little as one-third the cost of installing traditional skylights.

TIP:

Check your weather forecast the day before you begin a skylight installation to make sure there's no prediction of rain or high winds on the way!

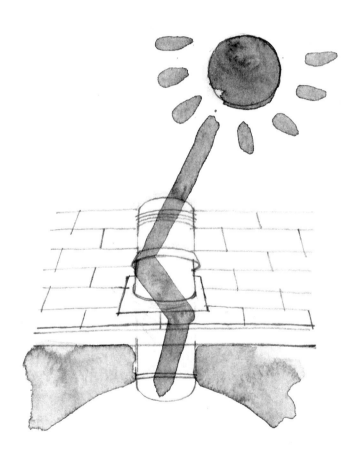

All-Out Excitement!

If you're blessed with the money, time, and patience, sometimes the best remodeling solution is simply to start from scratch. Rip off that cruddy countertop; ditch the dingy cabinets too, while you're at it!

And you don't have to stop the demolition derby there. Let yourself think outside the box—the four boxy walls of your existing kitchen, that is. Could you remove a partition wall that now separates your kitchen and dining room, or make better use of space by annexing an adjacent porch, closet or bath?

Adding space by adding on may also be an option—though probably not an inexpensive one! Check local zoning and setback regulations to be sure they will let you build "out" in the direction you want to go. For big projects like additions, you may be best advised to consult an architect or building designer to help you integrate the old and new spaces both structurally and aesthetically. Remember, too, that adding square footage may add value to your home, but it will also increase your taxes!

However you rearrange your kitchen space, one of the beauties of starting from scratch is it allows you to completely rethink existing traffic and work patterns. You're not stuck with doors where someone else put them. You can alter cabinet layouts and configurations, increase counter space, add a breakfast bar, or even incorporate an office or meal-planning nook.

TIP:

Planning a large-scale remodel? Don't forget to plan for plants! Think about where you might like to keep potted herbs or a favorite African violet—how big a space will you need? Will there be enough light for plants to thrive? How easy is it to water them? If your household includes pets, don't forget to include them in your planning, too! Can you create a spot for a bird perch, or build in a kitty condo/window seat? Could a lower drawer conceal Fido's food dishes? Do you need additional storage for bulk pet food?

Layout & Design Issues

You've probably run across the term "kitchen triangle"—a favorite concept with kitchen designers for nearly 50 years. Designers using this traditional approach would look at the

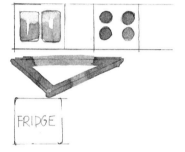

placement of the three major appliances: stove, refrigerator, and sink. The optimum "triangle" connecting these appliances was considered to be roughly 12 to 26 feet, with no single leg totaling more than about 9 feet.

The kitchen-triangle idea stood the test of time because it made sense: stove, fridge, and sink were the key elements of the traditional kitchen, and minimizing the number of steps that a cook had to take between them was a smart idea.

But today's kitchens function a whole lot differently than kitchens of the 1950s. For one thing, they often need to accommodate two working-parents-on-the-fly as cooks, rather than just one stay-at-home chef. Meals today are apt to include many more prepared, ready-to-cook, and reheat-and-serve ingredients. And we've grown to depend on a wider variety of kitchen appliances than we did in the I Love Lucy generation—from food processors to microwaves, from toaster ovens to juicers.

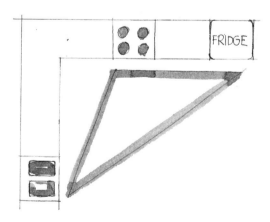

Reflecting the changing ways we use our kitchens, designers are shifting their emphasis to task-focused areas within the kitchen. Not that they're throwing the traditional "kitchen triangle" out the greenhouse window—far from it. But the buzz-phrase today is "work centers." And while you can slice the kitchen-work pie in any number of ways, here are three common design groupings:

✔ *Food preparation:* Refrigerator and counter space for chopping/mixing. Ideally contains at least a small sink. May include a separate chopping block.

✔ *Cooking station(s):* Range or cooktop. Ideally located near pots, pans, and utensils, and with a source of water nearby. (Because baking generally requires less "tending" than stovetop cooking, wall ovens may or may not be located immediately within this area.)

✔ *Cleanup:* Large sink, disposal, dishwasher, and related countertop space. Ideally, storage for cups, dishes and flatware is provided nearby.

TIPS FROM THE PROS:

"The kitchen, unfortunately, is too often designed around a footprint that was put in place in the 1930s and really hasn't changed much since. Standard dimensions such as 36-inch counters were intended for a 5-foot, 6-inch-tall woman. But users today are so varied! Now, we're trying to design kitchens for kids through the elderly; people of all shapes, sizes, and abilities—that's the idea behind 'universal design'. One of the ways of describing its aims that I really like is 'for a lifetime, rather than just your prime time.' The idea is to begin to build in some flexibility so we can make adjustments—just as life tends to do."

—Jane Langmuir, adjunct associate professor, Rhode Island School of Design

Layout Logic:

What height are normal countertops? How much space should you allow for a standard dishwasher or sink? You'll find the answers to those—and a long list of other questions—in the "Specs" appendix beginning on page 150.

Each family's kitchen needs and wants will be different, and there are a myriad of factors that will influence exactly what goes where. But here are some basic guidelines to keep in mind as you plan your new kitchen layout:

TIP:

Need to open up or move interior walls? Don't forget to insulate! No, interior insulation probably won't help much with your energy bill. But adding insulation to partition walls can significantly reduce noise transfer between rooms. (And if you're remodeling exterior walls, of course, insulation will be required for energy reasons.)

- ✎ Allow ample counter "landing" space at both ends of the sink, near the cooktop/range, and beside the handle ("opening") side of your refrigerator.
- ✎ Plan for plenty of outlets convenient to the locations where they'll be used. If your countertop will have an appliance garage, for example, include an adequate number of outlets inside the garage.
- ✎ Minimize the flow of traffic through your work area. Even though the kitchen-triangle concept isn't getting quite the attention it once did, it's still a good idea to treat the sink, fridge, and cooktop triangle as "holy ground," and to try to divert traffic away from it.
- ✎ If you'll have a cooktop, consider moving the wall oven—a "less-tended" appliance—away from the central work area.
- ✎ Allow at least a 36-inch work area for a small desk or office nook, and try to place it in AWAY from the main flow of traffic and as far as possible from dishwasher and sink to minimize noise and spills.

Sound a lot like the "fridge, range, and sink" elements of the old kitchen triangle? Well, yes and no. There's a lot more duplication in newer design configurations. The food prep station might include an under-counter refrigerated drawer for frequently used fresh fruits and vegetables, allowing the full-size refrigerator to be a few more steps away. Water may be available not only in one large cleanup sink, but in a smaller food-prep sink and perhaps even through a "pot-filler" spigot near the range, as well! There may even be multiple workstations for food prep or other functions. Cooks who do a lot of pie- and pastry-making, for example, may want to create a separate baking center—perhaps with a built-in marble slab and convenient storage for cookie sheets—in addition to a more generic food-preparation area. Standard kitchen layouts include:

The galley kitchen (one compact cousin: the single wall or Pullman kitchen). Most cooks find a galley layout pleasantly efficient and easy to work in—just turn around, and you're a step or two from another appliance or work area. (Single-wall kitchens, on the other hand, may require a few more steps to get from one end to the other, but are typically used only in small spaces anyway, which helps keep the number of steps to a minimum.) Through-traffic is often a concern with either galley-style or single-wall designs. And because the long walls are rather close and parallel, it's important to preserve a roomy aisle if possible, and to choose colors and features that foster a sense of openness. Appliances in galley kitchens are typically arranged with the sink and refrigerator on one wall, and the range opposite. For Pullman-style kitchens, the sink is frequently placed in the middle, with the refrigerator and range at the ends.

TIPS FROM THE PROS:

"A lot of people go for islands. Yes, they're lovely. But if there isn't counter space on either side of the cooktop, working on them can be a real pain! Remember that you'll need a place for tools, a spot to set pots. Just a stovetop in the middle of a tiny space doesn't work."

—*Chef Lisa Schroeder, Portland, Oregon*

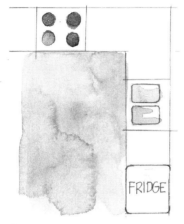

TIP:

Contemplating an island addition? Remember that an island doesn't always have to be square to the room—would an angle work better? Try different sizes and locations on your floor with masking tape (remember to include the counter overhang!) to see what works best.

The L-shaped kitchen. This flexible layout permits a compact work triangle, with the sink and range typically grouped on one leg and the refrigerator on the other. With the work area is tucked in its own corner, traffic flow is usually not a problem. But because this layout is so efficient, cabinet and counter space may be limited. If space permits, consider adding a breakfast bar or peninsula as an economical way to add extra space for counters, dining, and storage.

The U-shaped kitchen. Potentially one of the most user-friendly kitchen designs, a U-shaped kitchen can offer abundant counter and storage space while keeping work areas efficiently close to each other. And because the space is self-contained, through-traffic is usually not a problem. L-shaped kitchens are sometimes enlarged to create a U-shape as a way to remedy workspace and storage limitations.

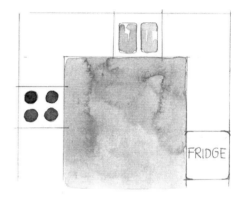

Islands are often added to enhance storage and counter space in either L-shaped or U-shaped kitchens, and to shorten steps between work areas. Many cooks find islands a terrific place to locate a second sink or cooktop. And with the addition of a simple overhang and some bar stools, one edge of the island can double as a casual dining area. But don't try to shoehorn an island in just for looks; islands generally work best in kitchens with at least 10 feet of open floor space between counters, and you should allow at least 42 inches for aisle width. Remember, too, that special downdraft ventilation will be required for such an installation. Similarly an island sink, though a marvelous convenience, will require its own plumbing runs.

universal Design

Imagine trying to fix dinner in your present kitchen if you had to do it from a wheelchair. Now imagine what it would be like if you also had limited manual dexterity or gripping strength. Could you reach cooking ingredients stored inside your cabinets, turn on the faucet, operate your cooktop's controls?

One of the most exciting trends in residential design work today is a philosophy called "universal design": creating spaces that work well for a wide range of users from very young children to aging grandparents, and of course people with varying physical abilities and limitations in between. It's a great idea whose time has come. And it's probably no coincidence that this focus on flexible living is emerging just as some 50 million baby boomers peer past their 50th birthdays!

Sure, universal design features can make kitchens easier to use for folks with physical limitations, and can allow the elderly to remain more independent. But in a testament to the power of good design, even people without mobility concerns report that spaces featuring these elements are easier and more pleasant to use. Here are some "universal-design" highlights for kitchens:

- Faucets are operated by a single control lever, rather than faucet knobs
- Wall switches and cooktop controls are placed lower for easy reach
- Hallways are wider, and contain no threshold at the doorway
- Sink base cabinet is left open to permit a wheelchair user to roll up to the edge
- Lighting and surfaces are designed for low-glare
- Countertop edges and cooktop controls use high-contrast colors for easy visibility
- Counters are provided at various heights to accommodate both tall and short cooks
- Cabinets feature pullout shelves
- Appliances are designed with easy-reach interiors (a microwave with a drop-down door; refrigerator shelves that are wide but less deep)

—Courtesy of Jane Langmuir, adjunct associate professor, Rhode Island School of Design

Do You Need More Amps?

We've probably all done the "dare I plug it in?" dance in a charmingly vintage kitchen—perhaps you're living with one of those now! If you're constantly blowing fuses when you try to run the toaster oven and dishwasher at the same time, you know exactly what I mean.

If you're contemplating a major kitchen remodel, now's the time to talk with an electrician about remedying that fuse-frying situation, once and for all. The solution is to run some additional circuits to your kitchen—and if you really do have fuses instead of circuit breakers, it's a good idea to modernize your panel anyhow.

How many kitchen circuits will you need? Check with your local building department for exact code requirements where you live. But here are some typical guidelines for new construction:

Lighting circuits: One (or if you have a really huge kitchen, maybe two) 15-amp circuits for kitchen lighting.

Outlets:

✔ Two 20-amp circuits for countertop outlets (plus one additional if you'll be plugging in a microwave larger than 1,000 watts)

✔ A separate 50-amp circuit (wired for 240 volts) for an electric cooktop, range, or wall oven

✔ A separate 20-amp refrigerator circuit

✔ A separate 20-amp circuit for the garbage disposal and dishwasher (in some areas, the dishwasher is required to be on its own circuit)

✔ One 15-amp circuit to run the clock and pilotless ignition system for a gas range

✔ A separate circuit for a trash compactor

Why do you need to count circuits? Each circuit requires its own circuit breaker, and there are a limited number of spaces available in a breaker-style service panel.

Once you determine how many circuits you'll need, your electrician will check to see whether there are enough vacant slots available in the existing service panel. If there's not enough room, he may be able to make do using space-saving "piggy-back" style breakers. Or you may need to upgrade your current service or install a subpanel.

Remember, too, that even if you have enough circuits to do the job, you may still be required to make some electrical upgrades to comply with current codes. Talk with your local building department about what you plan to change. If you'll be modifying countertop wiring, for example, they may insist that you add GFI (ground fault interrupt) protection to all counter-top outlets.

Electrical Conventions

The following are standard heights and dimensions for switch and outlet placement; you may wish to alter heights to accommodate the reach of disabled users. Always check with your local building department for exact local requirements.

- ✔ Countertop outlets are typically located 42 inches above the floor. Provide at least one outlet for each run of countertop section of greater than 12 inches, and space countertop outlets no more than 4 feet apart.
- ✔ Conventional switch height is 48 inches above the floor.
- ✔ Floor outlets are typically located 12 to 14 inches above the floor.

Cabinets

Unless you go hog wild over imported Italian tile and hand-sculpted marble countertops, cabinetry is probably going to be your largest single expense in an all-out kitchen remodeling. And your cabinets will also likely make the largest visual impact when the project is done. So it's important to choose carefully.

In the days before World War II, kitchen cabinets were crafted to the homeowner's specifications by a carpenter using milled lumber. Not anymore! Today's cabinets are more like a child's Lego set. They come as a series of different-size boxes that can be mixed and matched in a virtually unlimited number of ways. And while many do still contain solid wood faces and structural members, cabinet sides and shelves are often made from some variety of plywood or particleboard.

Choices in kitchen cabinetry are usually broken down as "stock," "semi-custom," and "custom" options. **Stock cabinets** are readily available (and often, yes, right in stock!) at your local home-improvement store. You'll be able to choose from a limited number of styles and finishes and pick a variety of standard layouts for each unit (including drawer units; sink base; corner units). Both base and upper cabinets come in graduated sizes (usually in 3-inch increments). "Filler" pieces can help adapt a cabinet run to virtually any space. Stock cabinets used to be sold as pre-assembled units; now, they're more apt to come in knocked-down ("ready to assemble") form. In addition to their affordable cost, stock cabinets offer one other potentially significant price advantage: if you have a truck, you can save added shipping costs. (Many stores also offer local delivery for a nominal charge.)

Semi-custom cabinets offer a wider selection of finishes, door styles, hardware, and other options, although again you'll be picking from

TIP:

A "filler strip" is often needed near corners to make sure appliances, cabinet doors and drawers have enough clearance to open properly.

a list of standard offerings from the manufacturer. Because these units must be specially ordered, expect to wait for delivery (one to two months is not unusual, though some manufacturers now promise delivery within 7-10 working days).

Custom cabinets are built by a local cabinetmaker or craftsman to your exact specifications. This will usually be the most expensive option, but you can get unusual woods, custom finishes, odd sizes or door arrangements tailored to your needs and wants. Timing (and cost) can be highly variable. Expect a wait of several months for the most in-demand craftsmen.

Details are what make the difference in quality cabinets. Drawer construction, in particular, can often provide important telltale clues: examine how the pieces are joined, check the materials used in slides and rollers. There's nothing quite as wonderful as the silky feel of a high-quality slide—or quite as irritating as a cheaply made drawer when the bottom gives out. High end lines may feature dovetailed joints; lower-quality drawers may be simply glued and stapled together. Also take a look at the cabinets' hinges, slides, and other hardware.

For years, oak was the fashion favorite for wood-faced cabinets. Though still popular, oak is facing increasingly stiff competition in the cabinet market from such woods as maple, cherry, birch, and pine, as well as a variety of tough, durable laminates. Today, most "wood" cabinets won't be made of solid wood, of course. But the better models will use sturdy plywood in cabinet backs, sides, and shelves rather than particleboard. A cabinet's finish will also be an indicator of quality. Less expensive models may have fewer coats of protective topcoat or may use low-pressure laminates (melamine) on shelving and sides.

Whiz-Bang Cabinet Extras:

Manufacturers are coming out with an increasing variety of "up and extra" options to help spice up cabinet arrangements. Some are available only on pricier models; others can be ordered for even the most basic stock cabinets. Here are just a few possibilities:

- ✔ Tambour "appliance garage"
- ✔ Glass or other specialty door fronts
- ✔ Vertical plate dividers
- ✔ Built-in wine rack or spice rack
- ✔ Pop-up electric mixer shelf
- ✔ Open-shelf upper cabinets for cookbooks, decorative pieces
- ✔ Knife drawer/cutting board
- ✔ Pullout shelves, Lazy Susans
- ✔ Recycling bin

**TIPS FROM
THE PROS:**

"Typically, we line up all the base cabinets along a wall, and fill them up with storage. But in the 'universal kitchen' I helped design, we have left two open spaces underneath the counter where you can store carts. A cart in the kitchen is an ideal component for multiple users because you can make a cart adjustable in height very easily, so it can be suited to the worker. It can be taken up to a counter's edge, and it can help you transfer heavy things or trash to various places. So it has many functions besides simply serving as a work space."

—*Jane Langmuir, adjunct associate professor, Rhode Island School of Design*

And what about style? Traditional kitchen cabinets use a face-framed design; that is, there's a narrow strip of wood around the opening of the cabinet box that provides both structural strength and a place to hang the doors. Euro-style cabinets, by contrast, feature "frameless" construction and concealed hinges. Cabinet doors and drawers fit flush with the edges of the cabinet box itself, for a smooth, uniform appearance. Euro design allows drawers and cabinet openings to be slightly larger. But because tolerances are so critical, Euro cabinets can be a challenge to install.

Some designers are breaking all the style rules by mixing and matching cabinet sizes, finish, colors and designs for an "unfitted" look. But remember: "eclectic chic" can be more difficult to pull off successfully than it appears in magazines! On the other hand, breaking with tradition can have its virtues. One relatively simple (and no-cost!) way to add interest to a plain cabinet layout: Simply stagger the MOUNTING heights of upper cabinets by several inches.

More Layout Logic

Whatever grade and style of cabinets you choose, it's important to consider carefully what sort of interior layout will serve you best. The same 72 inches of cabinet run can be made up with standard door/shelf units, drawer bases or a variety of combinations, for example.

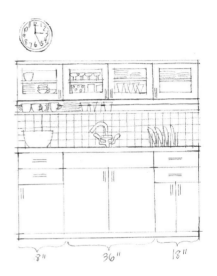

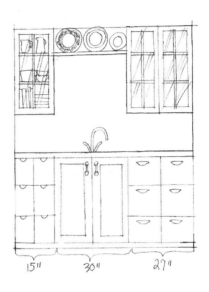

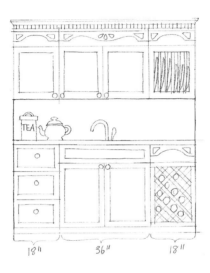

Most kitchen and home-improvement stores will offer help in planning before you buy or order. Or a bit of pencil pushing on your part may be all it takes.

One layout trend you may want to keep in mind: Drawers are becoming increasingly popular storage spots for everything from spices to stockpots. Some trendy homes are now being designed with base cabinets using almost exclusively drawers units, instead of shelves. And it's easy to—well, see why! A drawer's entire area is visible at a glance, and its ability to pull contents forward neatly eliminates the struggle to unearth items buried in the back. Still, not all drawer bases are equally useful. Because narrow drawers are less versatile, some designers recommend choosing a minimum drawer cabinet width of at least 18 inches.

Installing cabinets

Thinking about installing kitchen cabinets yourself? It's not as tough a job as you might think, although getting everything straight and level can take some time and tweaking.

Plan to line up a handy helper—preferably someone who's already done this task a time or two! Though most cabinets install in basically the same way, it's a good idea to read through the manufacturer's literature carefully before you begin. Some manufacturers even offer instructional videos—ask at the store where you're purchasing your cabinets.

Here are the basic steps to install kitchen cabinets:

1. Cabinets will be screwed to the wall and to each other. Begin by using a stud-finder to locate and mark the vertical studs in each wall where cabinets will attach.

2. Determine where the bottom edge of your upper cabinets will be located, and use a level to draw a horizontal line. Mount a temporary ledger strip (1x2 or 1x4) along this line to support and help align the upper cabinets.

3. Beginning with a corner unit, have your helper hold the first upper cabinet in place. Mark the stud's location; then pre-drill and screw the unit in place. (It may help to remove cabinet doors first.) Use a level to check cabinet alignment; shim as necessary to make straight and level. Then pre-drill and hang adjacent upper cabinets.

4. To install base cabinets, measure up 34 1/2 inches in several locations along the cabinet wall(s); use a level to determine which measurement is highest, and extend that line along the wall(s) of your base cabinet run. (NOTE: If you plan to lay new floor tile, it's usually best to do it before the cabinets are installed. If that's not possible, add the thickness of your future flooring to the 34 1/2-inch measurement to ensure the correct final counter height.)

5. Using shims if necessary, install the first (corner) base cabinet so that its top edge is even with your line. (For Lazy Susan models with no top lip, attach the corner unit to the two adjacent base cabinets and mount all three together.) Continue pre-drilling and mounting adjoining base units. Cut holes for plumbing and electrical access as necessary.

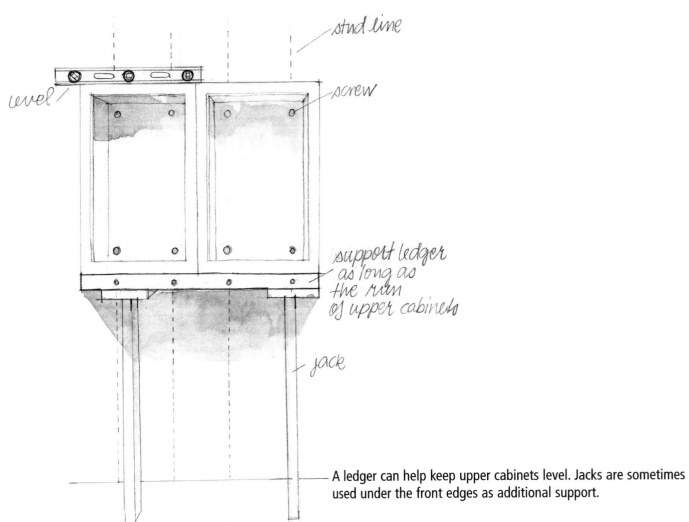

A ledger can help keep upper cabinets level. Jacks are sometimes used under the front edges as additional support.

Countertops

Choices in countertop materials have also burgeoned in recent years, thanks in large part to the continuing evolution of versatile, durable synthetic surfacing products.

Whatever the countertop material you choose, it can be a good idea to leave the measuring up to your fabricator or installer—so any errors are up to them to make good! And because house walls are often not perfectly square (and "as-built" dimensions may vary slightly from the plans), countertop installers will generally want to obtain exact measurements *after* base cabinets have been installed—a practical point which may translate into several weeks of trying to make do in a counterless kitchen. So be prepared!

Laminate: The most popular—and probably not coincidentally, frequently the most economical—choice for countertops are laminate materials. Made with resin-impregnated paper fused onto a plywood or particleboard base, laminates are grease-, stain-, and moisture-resistant. They're also easy to maintain—just wipe clean. And there's room to play when it comes to the details; laminates can be paired with a solid-surface or wood edging for contrast.

Though reasonably durable, laminate counters are not forever. Knives can nick them; hot pans can burn them; and over time, they may fade, chip, and (if water seeps in) even delaminate. Actual results, of course, will depend on how well you treat them. I've seen laminate counters in great condition after 15 years; others may be ready for replacing in just five to seven. For best performance, choose laminates with a non-glossy finish to help mute tiny wear and scratch marks. Some upper-end laminate products also offer a slightly thicker (1/16 inch) surface layer, which permits minor nicks to be sanded out.

Laminate counters can be custom-fabricated by kitchen-design companies or experienced contractors. It is possible to do countertop laminating yourself, although you'll need special tools to properly miter the joints. A little less imposing on the do-it-yourself scale are ready-to-install stock countertops (also known as "post-formed" tops). These economical laminate countertops are available in a limited assortment of colors and sizes at most home-improvement stores and can easily be cut to length. One word of caution from the voice of experience: Be careful transporting and handling post-formed tops, as too much pressure may crack the joint on the integral backsplash!

Ceramic Tile: It's heatproof, moisture-resistant, and highly durable. Little wonder that ceramic tile has long been a favorite for kitchen counters. Sure, you can crack or chip a tile if you're not careful. But treated properly, ceramic tile will earn its reputation for exceptional good looks and longevity.

Be sure to select a tile that's rated for countertop use, NOT a more delicate wall tile. And avoid extremes when it comes to the glazing: Porous, unglazed tile will require constant resealing, while tiles sporting a high-gloss shine will be notoriously unforgiving about minor scratches and wear.

Grout, of course, is the one blot on this near-perfect picture. While tile resists stains, grout seems to welcome them. And if tile is easy to keep clean, grout is anything BUT. Well, traditional grout, that is. Though not widely used, there are "epoxy"-type grouts now on the market that boast greatly improved stain-resistance. (Contractors, unfortunately, tend to shun them because they're a bit more difficult to work with. See sidebar.) And if you prefer to use traditional grout, an acrylic sealer can certainly help—just remember to reapply it as directed.

TIP:

You may be able to cut a deal on discontinued tile patterns and tile "seconds." Decorative tiles with minor flaws in the glazing or color may make fabulous (and inexpensive!) backsplash accents. Whether you purchase in-stock or discontinued patterns, always buy a few extra tiles for future repairs, "just in case!"

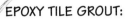 **EPOXY TILE GROUT:**

Hate dingy grout—but less than excited about those scrubbing sessions with toothbrush and bleach? Consider epoxy grout for your next tile job. Available at tile stores, epoxy offers a giant leap forward in grout toughness and stain-resistance. But even experienced tile-setters can find epoxy grout challenging to apply. Because hardening occurs chemically, proper mixing is crucial and there's a limited working window. (Pay special attention to manufacturers' recommendations about working temperatures!) And both grout application and cleanup require a little extra effort. It's from two to four times as expensive as regular grout—and worth every penny.

TIPS FROM THE PROS:

"I have wooden counters throughout my kitchen, and I love them. But they're not for everyone. Don't be too optimistic if you choose wood; know that they're going to take some care. I treat mine regularly with an expensive oil, but food, liquids, even silverware, will leave stains that take bleaching to really get out. You can't just swipe lightly with a sponge and expect your countertops to look perfectly clean."

—*Cindi Dixon, illustrator, photographer*

Butcher Block: Butcher block tops are also exceedingly popular for at least part of a countertop run. A butcher block section can provide a convenient and durable cutting surface. And the natural wood surface can even help dampen sound a bit.

Maple is the most popular choice for butcher block counters, though other hardwoods such as red or white oak, birch, and beech are also sometimes used. Butcher block tops will typically be 1 or 1 1/2 inches in thickness (the thicker the better for high-use areas), and come in standard 24-, 30- and 36-inch widths. Counters fabricated with the denser end-grain of the wood facing up will be more durable, but also more expensive than edge-grain or face-grain styles.

Butcher block counters can easily be cut to size, and installation is fairly straightforward (it's typically mounted from below with screws). Just remember to account for varying material thicknesses if you plan to blend butcher block and other types of surfacing on a continuous countertop run!

Because they're made of natural wood, butcher block countertops can burn, shrink, and crack if not properly protected. They're best used in areas away from excessive moisture or heat, and will require regular recoating with salad, mineral, or other nontoxic oil to prevent the wood from absorbing stains and odors. Check to see what your manufacturer recommends for products and maintenance schedule.

Solid-Surfacing: A relative newcomer to the countertop scene, solid surfacing materials are now second in popularity only to laminates. Like laminates, they offer easy cleanup—and the buff-able, color-through composition of solid surfacing takes durability up a notch. A number of makers now offer solid surfacing which (at a distance, anyhow) resembles granite, marble, ivory, and other exotic materials—at a much more affordable price.

Typically a blend of polyester resins and mineral fillers, solid surfacing can be formed, cut, routered and shaped, permitting a wide variety of decorative variations.

Counter edges can be sculpted, for example; contrasting color bands can be inlaid into countertop or backsplash; and seamless sinks can be molded right in.

Like anything else, solid surfacing does have its drawbacks. Though reasonably durable under ordinary use (many brands carry a 10-year warranty), solid surfacing won't stand up to harsh encounters with hot pans. And don't expect to be able to treat it as a cutting board! Dark colors may show nicks more readily.

Solid surfacing typically comes in sheets that are between 1/2 and 1 1/2 inches thick (thinner materials may require underlayment for structural support). For about half the price, you can opt for solid-surfacing veneer (SSV), available in sheets only 1/4 to 1/2 inch thick.

Installation of solid surfacing is NOT a do-it-yourself project; special tools, techniques, and training are required. (And many manufacturers refuse to guarantee the material's performance unless trained professionals have installed it.)

Because countertops must be custom-fabricated, expect an ordering delay of two weeks or longer.

TIP: Love the look of stone, but hyperventilating at the price tag? Consider using stone tiles rather than one solid piece on your countertop for a similarly elegant (but much more affordable!) effect.

Stone: Smoothly elegant, all-natural, and incredibly long wearing, stone makes a marvelous countertop material. But the price tag for this lavish look is not for the faint of heart!

If you decide to take the plunge, shop stone dealers early in the remodeling process to ensure material availability, and to schedule installation. Particularly with material this expensive, don't risk a transposed number or a misplaced sink cutout. Insist that the dealer take exact ordering measurements (after the cabinets are in!). Then double-check those dimensions yourself. Plan on a significant "counter-less" waiting period before the stone arrives; six to eight weeks is not unusual.

The two most popular stone countertop materials are granite and marble. Granite

TIP:

Many cooks enjoy the flexibility of MIXED countertop surfaces—perhaps colorful laminate with an inset marble baking slab in the pastry area, or a maple chopping block island to complement solid surfacing elsewhere in the kitchen. Just remember to adjust for varying thicknesses whenever dissimilar materials will be installed side-by-side.

is the harder and less porous of the two. It's heatproof, chip-proof, waterproof, and highly stain- and scratch-resistant. Its smooth, cool surface is also a natural for any cook who loves pastry making. And a bit of regular polishing is all that's needed to help maintain luster. But like most stone, the hard surface is unforgiving on breakables.

More porous than granite, marble must be sealed (and resealed!) to resist water damage and oil stains. And acid foods such as lemons and wine are no-nos—they can etch away the shine.

Other types of stone putting in an appearance on kitchen counters lately include soapstone, limestone, and slate. These interesting materials can offer more subtle coloration than granite or marble—but remember that their colors may darken when sealer is applied. And because they're somewhat softer and more porous than the harder stones, they're also slightly more prone to chips and stains.

Prices for a stone countertop will vary depending upon the type of material, coloration, and thickness. I'm sure I don't have to tell you that stone is heavy. So as you're pricing stone countertops, remember that cabinet bases may require additional reinforcement and shipping costs can be substantial.

Stainless: There's a reason that stainless-steel sinks and countertops have been preferred for years in institutional settings. Several reasons, actually! Stainless is exceptionally rugged, scratch-resistant, non-corroding, heatproof, and easy to clean. There's no protective coating to renew or maintain. Sinks and drainboards can be fabricated right into the countertop. And according to a recent study by the Hospitality Institute of Technology & Management in St. Paul, Minnesota, stainless-steel countertops are less likely to harbor such dangerous bacteria (E. coli, for instance) than other common countertop materials such as plastic laminates, wood, tile, granite, or concrete.

Like stone, however, custom-fabricated stainless countertops can cost a pretty penny. The heavier the gauge, the more expensive—and the more durable. Because it can dent, stainless must be installed over a supporting substrate such as plywood.

Concrete: It's a rather surprising role for this rough-and-ready building material. But if you think concrete is strictly for sidewalks, foundations, and building blocks, think again!

There's been a recent flurry of fascination with poured-concrete countertops. Tints or stains can transform its lackluster gray to solid colors, and the addition of chips of marble or glass can allow the blend to mimic stone. Sinks and drainboards can be formed in seamlessly. Even the final finish is more flexible than you might think; concrete counters can be smoothed and polished to a high-gloss shine, or left sandstone-rough.

Though strong, durable, and scratch-resistant, concrete will tend to develop hairline cracks over time (though they're generally considered "part of the charm"). Concrete's surface must be sealed and waxed regularly to maintain its appearance and prevent stains. Cabinet bases may need reinforcing to bear the considerable weight. And despite concrete's rather homespun reputation, unless you do it yourself, these countertops may NOT be cheap! Materials alone may cost as little as $500. But the final cost for labor and materials can be nearly equal to that of stone, and contractors with experience in this rather new field may be difficult to find.

Conclusion

We hope we've given you some great remodeling ideas—and perhaps even the inspiration to tackle some of the work yourself!

TIP:

Ah, the great garbage dilemma! You probably don't want to leave an unsightly can out in the open—but stooping to open a cabinet and reach inside all the time is hardly convenient, either! One of the cleverest solutions I've seen: a garbage chute! This particular creative genius sliced the bottom off a round metal sherbet container, and then set it in a hole in the countertop directly above his garbage can. The easily-cleanable tube funnels kitchen waste directly into the waiting container below. And the canister lid neatly covers the opening when not in use.

Here's a coffee cup toast to your new kitchen, with fond hopes that you, too, will always find it full of good friends, good company, good conversation—and of course, great food!

Biographies

Eva Bender:
Eva Bender is a fine artist and watercolorist who exhibits her paintings regularly in Sweden and Lancaster, Pennsylvania. Eva recently redid her charming cottage kitchen to include a period tongue-in-groove ceiling.

Rose Levy Beranbaum:
Author of seven cookbooks, including *The Pie and Pastry Bible* (Scribner, 1998) and *The Cake Bible* (Wm. Morrow, 1988), which was designated Cookbook of the Year by the International Association of Culinary Professionals/Seagram. Rose recently completed a successful renovation of her own kitchen and credits her contractor's enthusiasm and sense of humor for helping "keep me sane during the six months that the center of my working life was in utter disarray!" Her new kitchen, complete with granite countertops and padded dental assistant's stool, was featured in the Christmas issue of *Home Magazine* in November, 1994.

Marie Cappuccio:
Marie is that rarity among attorneys—smart, beautiful, warm, honest, compassionate. To the great dismay of her devoted clients, she hopes to soon close her law office in Hammonton, New Jersey after 18 years of practice to write, travel, and savor life with her husband, Marc.

Julia Child:
Her name has become a household word. But in case you've been living under a rock for the past three decades, Mrs. Child is the author of *The French Chef Cookbook* (30th Anniversary Edition, 1998), and host of the "Master Chef" and "Baking at Julia's" television series plus the new PBS "Julia and Jacques Cooking at Home" show. She is also just as warm and witty, caring and candid when she speaks to you in person as she sounds on television.

Ann Cooper:
Author of *A Woman's Place Is In The Kitchen* (Wiley, 1997) and *Bitter Harvest: A Chef's Perspective on the Dangers of Our Food Supply* (Routledge, 2000), Ann is a corporate chef for The Putney Inn in Vermont; an industry services consultant with the Culinary Institute of America; and executive chef for the Telluride Film Festival.

Cindi Dixon:
Cindi Dixon is a fine artist and former fashion illustrator. She is in increasing demand for her stunning black-and-white wedding photography. Cindi has renovated several houses, and notes that work on her current three-story Victorian home "will never be finished!" Her photography studio, Silver Studios, is based in Lancaster, Pennsylvania.

Meredith Gould:
Author of *Working At Home* (Storey Books, 2000) and *Staying Sober: Tips for Working a Twelve-Step Program of Recovery* (Hazelden, 1999). Based in Princeton, New Jersey, Gould is an editor and in her role as organizing guru "Space Queen," helps the busy and befuddled tidy up. She can be reached via e-mail: SpaceQueen@compuserve.com.

Helen Jay:
Helen is the author of *Paper Dragons, Journey to the Shamanic Roots of Feng Shui* (China Studio, 2000) and with her husband James Jay, co-director of the Feng Shui Designs Learning Center in Nevada City, California. More information about the Learning Center and the principles of Feng Shui is available at their website, www.fsdi.com.

Michael Lamb:
Michael is a certified energy manager with the Energy Efficiency & Renewable Energy Clearinghouse in Merrifield, Virginia. He has worked in the construction industry for 20 years as an electrician, plumber, and carpenter, and "always had a yen for energy conservation."

Jane Langmuir:
Jane is an adjunct associate professor at Rhode Island School of Design's interior architecture department in Providence, Rhode Island. She was project director of the five-year project "Universal Kitchen" at RISD. Two kitchen prototypes from the project have been exhibited at the Smithsonian's Cooper-Hewitt National Design Museum and the Kitchen and Bath Show in Orlando.

Lesley Morrison:
My younger sister, Lesley has applied her terrific taste to repainting and papering at least 4 houses and somehow managed to keep her patience and sense of humor intact (a talent no doubt honed in childhood by learning to put up with me!).

Michael Pantano:
Michael is a commercial kitchen planner and partner in Culinary Advisors, a commercial foodservice facility planning firm in Ellicott City, Maryland. The current president of the Foodservice Consultants' Society International, Michael has been known to address stuffy professional gatherings with a large can prominently labeled "Worms" on the podium.

Ann F. Potter:
Independent chef Ann F. Potter has worked for the CEOs of such major corporations as Dana Corp. of Toledo, Ohio; Owens-Corning; Calphalon Corp; and Wilcox Financial, and has worked in every facet of the restaurant business over the past 20 years. She is presently based in San Antonio, Texas, but notes "Have knives, will travel!"

Lisa Schroeder:
Formerly a chef at New York's famous Le Circque and Lespinasse restaurants, Lisa is now owner of her own resturant, Mother's Bistro & Bar in Portland, Oregon, and "in the throes" of remodeling her own kitchen.

B. Smith:
Lifestyle expert B. Smith does it all—and all with her signature flair for "style"! One smile and your feel like you've been invited into her kitchen—and her heart. She is the author of *B. Smith's Entertaining and Cooking for Friends* (Artisan, 1995) and *B. Smith: Rituals and Celebrations* (Random House, 1999), host of the nationally syndicated TV show "B. Smith With Style," and editor-in-chief of *B. Smith Style* magazine.

Joan Stanford:
Joan and her husband Jeff are co-owners of the nearly-magical Stanford Inn, a 33-room hotel with certified organic gardens and a lavish all-vegetarian restaurant in Mendocino, California. But their first foray into the inn-keeping business was on a somewhat smaller scale. "We started out living in a room behind the office, so our personal kitchen was the same as for the inn—and our children were there, too. It was very tiny, but it worked!" she says.

Glossary

BTU (British Thermal Unit)
A measure of heat (to be precise, one BTU is the amount of heat required to raise one pound of water one full degree Fahrenheit!)

Change order
An alteration to a construction contract, typically after the project is already under way, specifying work or materials to be added or deleted.

Convection
A baking technology that uses circulating air to cook foods in less time than typically required with conventional ovens.

Face-framed cabinets
A traditional cabinet construction style in which doors are mounted to a narrow "frame" circling the cabinet opening.

Frameless cabinets
A more modern or "European" style of cabinets, in which doors are fit flush with the edges of the cabinet box.

Laminate
A type of building material in which two or more layers are bonded together by heat, pressure, glue, or a combination of those methods.

Low-e coating
An extremely thin metallic coating applied to one side of a window's glass by the manufacturer to reduce the transfer of heat (the term stands for "low emissivity").

Punch list
A final "to-do" list compiled by the homeowner or project foreman and given to the contractor to complete (typically, before final payment).

R-value
A measure of a window's resistance to heat transfer (higher numbers are associated with higher-quality windows).

Retention
A portion of the contract price which is "held back" until the work is satisfactorily completed.

SHGC
"Solar heat gain coefficient" is a measure of a window's shading properties, using a decimal scale from zero to one. (Zero represents a totally blocked window, while one is the equivalent of an untinted pane of glass.)

Solid-surfacing
A type of countertop material composed of polyester resin and mineral filler, typically offering a "flecked" appearance resembling granite and other exotic natural materials.

Sones
A measure of noise.

U-value
The reciprocal of "R-value," U-value measures the amount of heat that can escape through a window (in general, a lower U-value indicates a higher-quality window).

Universal design
Design principles that accentuate accessibility and ergonomics to allow a room to function well for a wide range of people of varying ages and physical abilities.

Specs, Specs, Nothing but the Specs!

Looking for some rules of thumb? The "bible" for kitchen dimensions and clearances are issued by the National Kitchen & Bath Association. Here are a few standard dimensions from their kitchen planning guidelines:

General layout:

- Configure work triangle at a total of 26 feet or less, with no single leg shorter than 4 feet or longer than 9 feet.

- Locate the dishwasher within 36 inches of the edge of the sink.

Walkways:
- In general, walkways should be at least 36 inches wide.
- For a one-cook kitchen, allow an aisle in central work area of at least 42 inches; allow 48 inches for multi-cook kitchens.
- No major traffic pattern should cross the work triangle.
- Provide at least 21 inches clear floor space beside the edge of the dishwasher for standing room while loading and unloading.

Countertops:

- Allow a total of at least 11 feet (132 inches) of usable counter frontage (kitchens over 150 sq. feet: at least 16 1/2 feet (198 inches), providing a minimum of 36 inches of continuous counter work space, preferably near the sink, for food-prep.
- Allow at least 24 inches on one side of the primary sink, and 18 inches on the other side. For a secondary sink, those clearances can be reduced to 18 inches and 3 inches.
- Provide at least 15 inches of "landing space" near regular and microwave oven, and on latch side of refrigerator.
- Provide two work heights: one 28–36 inches and the other 36–45 inches above the floor.
- Allow at least 24 inches between a cooking surface and a protected surface above (30 inches for unprotected surface).

Cabinets:

- Small kitchens (under 150 sq. feet) should have a total of at least 12 feet (144 inches) of wall cabinet and 13 feet (156 inches) base cabinet frontage; larger kitchens should include at least 15 feet (186 inches) of wall cabinet and 16 feet (192 inches) of base cabinet frontage.
- To accommodate cooks with disabilities, provide knee space 27 inches high by 30 inches wide by 19 inches deep near sinks, cooktops, ranges and ovens.

Note: Dimensions courtesy of the National Kitchen & Bath Association. For further information or for their complete list of kitchen planning guidelines, please contact the NKBA at (800) 843-6522 or visit their Web site at www.nkba.com.

Typical Appliance Widths & Other Dimensions:

Note: While these are common dimensions, your mileage may vary! Always measure your own appliances and cabinets carefully before beginning your kitchen planning.

- **Refrigerator:** 36 inches
- **Dishwasher:** 24 inches
- **Microwave:** 24 inches
- **Range:** 30 inches
- **Cooktop:** 36 inches
- **Double-bowl sink:** 36 inches
- **Base cabinet:** 24 inches deep and 34 inches high, which allows for a finished counter height of 36 inches.
- **Wall cabinet:** 12 inches deep and 30 inches high, mounted 15 to 18 inches above the countertop (25 inches above an island, or 30 inches above cooktop).

Sources & Resources

The following sources should give you a good starting place for many product, installation and safety questions. While we've tried to include a wide variety of useful sources, it's obviously impossible to list every quality manufacturer or helpful hotline. To anyone who may be left out, our apologies!

Please note: Inclusion on this list is NOT intended as a product endorsement or recommendation of any kind.

APPLIANCES:

AGA Cookers
(800) 633-9200; (770) 438-9150
6400 Highlands Pkwy #F
Smyrna, GA 30082
www.aga-cookers.com

Amana
(800) 843-0304
2800 220th Trail
Amana, IA 52204
www.amana.com

ASKO
(800) 367-2444 for brochures or
(972) 238-0794 customer service
1161 Executive Drive West
Richardson, TX 75081
www.askousa.com

Bosch Home Appliance
(800) 866-2022
2800 S. 25th Avenue
Broadview, IL 60153
www.bosch.com

Broan
(800) 558-1711
P.O. Box 140
Hartford, WI 53027
www.broan.com

Dacor
(800) 772-7778 to locate dealer;
(800) 793-0093 corporate offices
950 S. Raymond Avenue
Pasadena, CA 91109
www.dacorappl.com

Fisher & Paykel
(888) 936-7872
22982 Alcalde Drive #201
Laguna Hills, CA 92653
http://usa.fisherpaykel.com

Frigidaire
(800) 374-4432 automated;
(706) 860-4110 customer assistance
P.O. Box 212378
Augusta, GA 30917
www.frigidaire.com

Frigo Design
(800) 836-8746
5860 McKinley Rd.
Brewerton, New York 13029
Makes custom appliance panel and trim kits to reface refrigerators, dishwashers, etc. in brushed aluminum, a wide variety of colored acrylic, and other materials.
www.frigodesign.com

Gaggenau
(800) 828-9165
5551 McFadden Avenue
Huntington Beach CA 92649
www.gaggenau.com/us/index.htm

General Electric (GE)
(800) 626-2000
9500 Williamsburg Plaza
Louisville, KY 40222
www.ge.com

Jenn-Air
(800) 688-1100
403 W. 4th Street North
Newton, IA 50208
www.jennair.com

KitchenAid
(800) 422-1230
553 Benson Road
Benton Harbor, MI 49022
www.KitchenAid.com

Maytag
(800) 688-9900
403 W. 4th Street North
Newton, IA 50208
www.maytag.com

Miele
(800) 289-6435
9 Independence Way
Princeton, NJ 08540
www.mieleusa.com

Sears Appliances
(800) 349-4358
P.O. Box 3671
Des Moines, IA 50322
In addition to selling many
brands of appliances, offers a
"Parts Direct" service with parts
from over 400 manufacturers,
including many items dating
back 10 years or more. Call
(800) 366-PART (7278) or visit
the Sears website and click on
"Parts."
www.sears.com

SubZero
(800) 222-7820
Box 44130
Madison, WI 53744-4130
www.subzero.com

Thermador
(800) 656-9226
5551 McFadden Ave
Huntington Beach, CA 92649
www.thermador.com

Viking
(888) VIKING1 (845-4641)—
automated literature request or
(601) 455-1200
Box 8012
Greenwood, MS 38930
www.viking-range.com

Whirlpool
(800) 253-1301
553 Benson Road
Benton Harbor, MI 49022
www.whirlpool.com

CABINETS & CABINET DOORS/REFACING:

Aristokraft, Inc.
(812) 482-2527
1 Aristokraft Sq.
P.O. Box 420
Jasper, IN 47547-0420
www.aristokraft.com

IKEA
(800) 434-4532 to request catalog or place order
IKEA H.Q./North America
Plymouth Commons
496 W. Germantown Pike
Plymouth Meeting, PA 19462
www.ikea-usa.com

Kitchen Cabinet Manufacturers Assn
(703) 264-1690
1899 Preston White Drive
Reston, VA 20191-5435
www.kcma.org

KraftMaid Cabinetry
(800) 571-1990 to locate dealer
in your area; (440) 632-5333 for
customer relations
15535 South State Ave.
P.O. Box 1055
Middlefield, OH 44062
www.kraftmaid.com

Merillat Industries
(800) 575-8763 for literature or
to be directed to a regional customer service number
P.O. Box 1946
Adrian, MI 49221
www.merillat.com

Quality Doors
(800) 950-DOOR (3667) or
(972) 291-2424
621 Hall Street
Cedar Hill, TX 75104

Raintree Kitchens Ltd.
(800) 217-9438 or (604) 513-
2292
18563 97th Ave
Surrey, BC CANADA V4N 3N9
Offers environmentally-friendly
cabinets made from a pressed-
wood alternative with virtually
no formaldehyde off-gassing.
www.raintree-kitchens.com

SieMatic
(800) 734-2665 for showroom
near you; (215) 244-6800
Two Greenwood Square
3331 Street Road #450
Bensalem, PA 19020
www.siematic.com

Wellborn Cabinet, Inc
(800) 336-8040; (800) 762-
4475; (205) 354-7151
P.O. Box 1210
Ashland, AL 36251
www.wellborncabinet.com

Woodharbor Doors & Cabinetry
(515) 423-0444
3277 Ninth Street SW
Mason City, IA 50401
www.woodharbor.com

Yorktowne Cabinets
(800) 777-0065
P.O. Box 231
Red Lion, PA 17356
www.yorktowneinc.com

COUNTERTOP MATERIALS:

Custom Building Products
(800) 272-8786
13001 Seal Beach Blvd
Seal Beach, CA 90740
Tile-related products such as
grout, sealers, etc.
www.custombuildingproducts.com

DuPont (Corian)
800/4-CORIAN (426-7426)
Box 80112
Wilmington, DE 19880
www.dupont.com/corian

Dakota Granite
(800) 843-3333; (605) 432-5580
301 S. Main Street
P.O. Box 1305
Millbank, SD 57252
www.dakgran.com

Dal-Tile
(800) 933-TILE (8453)
7834 C.F. Hawn Freeway
Dallas, TX 75217
www.daltile.com;
www.aotile.com

Florida Tile
(800) 789-TILE (8453)
P.O. Box 447
Lakeland, FL 33802
www.floridatile.com

Formica Corp.
(800) 367-6422 for product info,
samples, dealer near you; (513)
786-3400 U.S. corporate head-
quarters
10155 Reading Rd.
Cincinnati, OH 45241
www.formica.com

Marble Institute of America
(614) 228-6194
30 Eden Alley #301
Columbus, OH 43215
Offers care and cleaning tips,
guidelines for residential counter
installations, etc.
www.marble-institute.com

Michigan Maple Block Co.
(800) 678-8459; (231) 347-4170
P.O. Box 245
Petoskey, MI 49770
Cutting boards, counter tops,
tables, and fast-drying synthetic
oil approved for use on food surfaces.
www.mapleblock.com

Syndesis
(310) 829-9932
2908 Colorado Avenue
Santa Monica, CA 90403-3616
Maker of precast cement surfacing material called Syndecrete,
with 41% recycled content.
www.syndesisinc.com

Technistone
(651) 351-3185
2403 Northridge Ave #N
Stillwater, MN 55082
Engineered stone made with
93% natural quartz sand aggre-
gate that's hard as granite yet
four times more flexible, and virtually maintenance-free.
www.technistone.com

Vermont Soapstone
(802) 263-5404
P.O. Box 268
248 Stoughton Pond Road
Perkinsville, VT 05151-0268
www.vermontsoapstone.com

Wilsonart International
(800) 433-3222
2400 Wilson Place
P.O. Box 6110
Temple, TX 76503
www.wilsonart.com

CRAFTS:

Michaels
(800)-MICHAELS (642-4235)
to locate a store near you; (972)
409-1300 corporate HQ
P.O. Box 619566
Dallas-Ft. Worth, TX 75261-
9566
www.michaels.com

Polyform Products
(847) 427-0020
1901 Estes
Elk Grove Village, IL 60007
Makers of Super Sculpey and
other craft clay products
www.sculpey.com

ENERGY SAVING RESOURCES, ENVIRONMENTAL ISSUES & "GREEN" BUILDING MATERIALS:

American Council for an Energy Efficient Economy
(202) 429-0063 for publications;
(202) 429-8873 research & conferences
1001 Connecticut Avenue NW #801
Washington, DC 20036
Publications include Consumer Guide to Home Energy Savings ($8.95, 273 pp.)
www.aceee.org

Center for Renewable Energy and Sustainable Technology (CREST)
(202) 293-2898
1612 "K" Street NW #410
Washington, DC 20006
www.solstice.crest.org

NCAT Center for Resourceful Building Technology
(406) 549-7678
P.O. Box 100
Missoula, MT 59806
Consulting on sustainable building materials and techniques; product guides and information.
www.montana.com/crbt or www.ncat.org

Certified Forest Products Council
(503) 590-6600
14780 SW Osprey Drive #285
Beaverton, OR 97007
www.certifiedwood.org

The Energy Efficiency & Renewable Energy Clearinghouse (EREC)
(800) DOE-EREC (363-3732)
P.O . Box 3048
Merrifield, VA 22116
Free general and technical information on many topics about energy efficiency, selecting appliances, and renewable energy.
www.eren.doe.gov; select Consumer Info link

Energy Efficient Lighting Association
(609) 799-4900
P.O. Box 727
Princeton Junction, NJ 08550
Promotes the purchase and installation of energy efficient lighting products.
www.eela.com

Energy Star Hotline
(888) 782-7937 (STAR-YES)
A collaborative effort by the U.S. Department of Energy, the U.S. Environmental Protection Agency, and manufacturers; includes a voluntary product labeling program for products which exceed minimum federal energy standards or offer special energy-saving features.
www.energystar.gov

Environmental Building News
(800) 861-0954 subscriptions;
(802) 257-7300
E Build Inc.
122 Birge Street #30
Brattleboro, VT 05301
Leading newsletter on environmentally responsible design and construction techniques. Also offers information on green building materials.
www.ebuild.com

Environmental Protection Agency
(800) 490-9198
Over 8,000 free consumer booklets including information about asbestos in the home and lead hazards.
www.epa.gov

Green Building Program
(512) 499-7827 general info
(512) 505-3706 publications
One of the best-known sustainable building programs, this one in Austin, Texas began in 1991 and now offers consulting nationwide to builders, architects and government agencies interested in sustainable building programs and practices.
www.ci.austin.tx.us/greenbuilder

Green Seal
(202) 872-6400
1001 Connecticut Avenue NW #827
Washington, DC 20036-5525
Independent, non-profit organization that promotes the manufacture and sale of environmentally-responsible products. Also issues newsletter ("Choose Green Reports") 8 times/year, $125 annual subscription or $25 per issue.
www.greenseal.org

Home Energy magazine
(510) 524-5405
2124 Kittredge Street PMB #95
Berkeley, CA 94704
A bi-monthly magazine offering information on home performance topics from air quality to energy efficient construction. Subscription $49 per year ($39 on the web).
www.homeenergy.org/magazine.html

Iris Communications Inc.
(800) 346-0104
P.O. Box 5920
Eugene, OR 97405-0911
Books, videos, and product information on sustainable building materials. Free catalog.
www.oikos.com

Lawrence Berkeley National Laboratory's Building Technology Program
(510) 486-6845
Windows & Daylighting Group
Mail Stop 90-3111
Berkeley, CA 94720
One of the nation's foremost authorities on windows and daylighting.
http://eetd.lbl.gov/BT.html

National Renewable Energy Laboratory
(303) 275-4363 documents
1617 Cole Blvd.
Golden, CO 80401-3393
A DOE national laboratory. Publishes consumer guides including "Buildings That Save Money With Efficient Lighting" and "Energy-Efficient Lighting."
www.nrel.gov

Raintree Kitchens Ltd.
(see entry under "Cabinets")

Rocky Mountain Institute
(970) 927-3851
1739 Snowmass Creek Road
Snowmass, CO 81654-9199
A non-profit research and educational organization promoting sustainable resource use. Publishes a newsletter and "Home Energy Briefs," plus other publications on a variety of topics.
www.rmi.org

FAUCETS:

American Standard
(800) 223-0068 technical questions; (800) 524-9797 catalogs & literature
U.S. Plumbing Products
P.O. Box 6820
Piscataway, NJ 08855-6820
www.us.amstd.com

Chicago Faucets
(800) 566-2100; (847) 803-5000
2100 S. Clearwater Drive
Des Plaines, IL 60018-5999
www.chicagofaucets.com

Delta Faucet Co.
(800) 345-DELTA (3358)
55 East 111th Street
P.O. Box 40980
Indianapolis, IN 46280
www.deltafaucet.com

Eljer
(800) 423-5537
14801 Quorum Drive
Addison, TX 75246-7584
mailing: P.O. Box 709001
Dallas, TX 75370-9998
www.eljer.com

The Faucet Outlet
(800) 444-5783
P.O. Box 547
Middletown, NY 10940
Over 38,000 kitchen and bath products from leading manufacturers, with photo and product information.
www.faucet.com

Kallista Inc.
(888) 452-5547 customer service; (888) 4KALLISTA literature
(a division of Kohler Co.)
2446 Verna Ct.
San Leandro, CA 94577-4223
www.kallistainc.com

Kohler Plumbing
(800) 4KOHLER customer service; (800) 456-4537 literature
444 Highland Drive
Kohler, WI 53044
www.kohlerco.com

KWC Faucets Inc.
(888) 592-3287; (678) 334-2121
1770 Corporate Drive #580
Norcross, GA 30093
www.kwcfaucets.com

Moen Inc.
(800) BUY-MOEN (289-6636)
25300 Al Moen Drive
North Olmsted, OH 44070-8022
www.moen.com

Peerless Faucet Co.
(800) GET-MORE (438-6673);
(317) 848-1812
55 E. 111th Street
Indianapolis, IN 46280
www.peerless-faucet.com

Price Pfister
(800) 732-8238; (818) 896-1141
13500 Paxton Street
Pacoima, CA 91333-4518
www.pricepfister.com

FLOORING:

Armstrong
(800) 233-3823; (717) 397-0611
2500 Columbia Avenue (17603)
P.O. Box 3001
Lancaster, PA 17604
www.armstrong.com

Award Hardwood Floors
(888) 870-7705
401 N. 72nd Avenue
Wausau, WI 54403
www.awardfloors.com

Bruce Hardwood Floors
(800) 722-4647
16803 Dallas Parkway
Dallas, TX 75248
www.brucefloors.com

Congoleum
(800) 934-3567 literature or
(800) 274-3266 consumer hotline
P.O. Box 3127
Mercerville, NJ 08619-0127
www.congoleum.com

Formica Flooring
(800) 367-6422
10155 Reading Road
Cincinnati, OH 45241
www.formica.com

Matrix Composites, Inc.
(800) 767-4495
6310 Shawson Drive
Mississauga, Ontario CANADA
L5T 1H5
www.solidsurfaceflooring.com or
www.materatile.com

Wilsonart International
(800) 433-3222
2400 Wilson
Placewww.wilsonart.com
P.O. Box 6110
Temple, TX 76503
www.wilsonart.com

FURNITURE & KITCHEN GADGETS:

Container Store
(800) 733-3532
2000 Valwood Pkwy
Dallas, TX 75234
www.containerstore.com

Crate & Barrel
(800) 967-6696
1860 W. Jefferson Avenue
Naperville, IL 60540
www.crateandbarrel.com

Hold Everything
(800) 421-2264 to order; (800)
421-2285 customer service
c/o Williams-Sonoma Inc.
3250 Van Ness Avenue
San Francisco, CA 94109
www.holdeverything.com

Kitchen & Home
(800) 646-5522
P.O. Box 2527
La Crosse, WI 54602-2527
www.kitchenandhome.com

Pottery Barn
(800) 922-5507 to order; (800)
922-9934 customer service
c/o Williams-Sonoma Inc.
3250 Van Ness Avenue
San Francisco, CA 94109
www.potterybarn.com

Sauder Woodworking
(800) 523-3987
P.O. Box 156
Archbold, OH 43502-0156
www.sauder.com

Solutions
(800) 821-1279 or (800) 342-9988
P.O. Box 6878
Portland, OR 97228-6878
www.solutionscatalog.com
Williams-Sonoma
(800) 541-2233 to order; (800)
541-1262 customer service
3250 Van Ness Avenue
San Francisco, CA 94109
www.williams-sonoma.com

KNOBS & PULLS:

Amerock Corp
(800) 618-9559; (815) 969-6308
4000 Auburn St.
P.O. Box 7018
Rockford, IL 61125-7018
Whimsical knobs and pulls
including knife, fork, spoon,
chili pepper, and pea pod shapes
in chrome or brass finishes.
www.amerock.com

Get A Grip
(303) 985-8081 for the dealer
nearest you
828 West Iliff Lane
Lakewood, CO 80227
Hand-crafted fine hardware
including western and modern
glass-and-chrome motifs
www.globalinc.com/getagrip

Hob Knobs
(888) 367-5662; (770) 631-4080
156 Peachtree East PMB #176
Peachtree City, GA 30269
Decorative 3-dimensional resin
knobs, handmade by a woman-
owned business.
www.hobknobsinc.com

LIGHTING:

American Lighting Association
(800) 274-4484 to locate show-room near you
P.O. Box 420288
Dallas, TX 75342-0288
Trade organization for lighting manufacturers and distributors. Offers helpful brochures ($2) on kitchen, bath, and other lighting applications, plus free tips online.
www.americanlightingassoc.com

The Brass Light Gallery
(800) 243-9595
131 S. First Street
Milwaukee, WI 53204
Hand-assembled reproduction brass fixtures in a variety of architectural styles.
www.brasslight.com

Energy Efficient Lighting Association
(609) 799-4900
P.O. Box 727
Princeton Junction, NJ 08550
Promotes the purchase and installation of energy efficient lighting products.
www.eela.com

Georgia Custom Lighting
(770) 963-6221
Box 325
Lawrenceville, GA 30246

Halo/Cooper Lighting
Customer Service: (770) 486-4800
1121 Highway 74 South

Peachtree City, GA 30269
Corporate offices: (847) 956-8400
400 Busse Rd
Elk Grove Village, IL 60007-2195
www.cooperlighting.com

Illuminating Engineering Society of North America
(212) 248-5000
120 Wall Street, 17th Floor
New York, NY 10005-4001
An association of lighting professionals.
www.iesna.org

Lighting Research Center
(518) 276-8716
Rensselaer Polytechnic Institute
110 - 8th Street, Watervliet Facility
Troy, NY 12180-3590
The world's largest university-based center for lighting research and education. Offers books and technical reports on home and energy-efficient lighting.
www.lre.rpi.edu

National Lighting Bureau
(301) 587-9572; (800) 854-7179 to order publications
8811 Colesville Road #G-106
Silver Spring, MD 20910
Industry trade group; offers consumer publications such as Getting the Most From Your Lighting Dollar ($15).
www.nlb.org

Period Lighting Fixtures
(800) 828-6990; (413) 664-7141
167 River Road
Clarksburg, MA 01247
Handmade reproductions of fixtures from the 1620s to 1850s.
www.periodlighting.com

Progress Lighting
(864) 599-6000
P.O. Box 5704
Spartanburg, SC 29304-5704
The largest residential lighting manufacturer in North America.
www.progresslighting.com

Rejuvenation Lamp & Fixture Co.
(888) 401-1900 to order; (888) 343-8548 catalog request; (503) 231-1900
2550 NW Nicolai Street
Portland, OR 97210
Authentic reproduction Victorian, Arts & Crafts, and other vintage-style fixtures.
www.rejuvenation.com

W.A.C. Lighting Co.
(800) 526-2588
615 South Street
Garden City, NY 11530
www.waclighting.com

ORGANIZERS:

(SEE ALSO Furniture & Kitchen Gadgets listings)

California Closets
(800) 2SIMPLIFY (274-6754)
20450 - 84th Avenue South
Kent, WA 98032
www.cclosets.com

ClosetMaid
(800) 874-0008
P.O. Box 4400
Ocala, FL 34478-4400
www.closetmaid.com

LeeRowan
(800) 325-6150
900 S. Highway Drive.
Fenton, MO 63026
www.leerowan.com

Tupperware
(800) 366-3800
P.O. Box 2353
Orlando, FL 32802
www.tupperware.com

PAINT:

Benjamin Moore
(800) 826-2623 to locate store
near you or (800) 344-0400
51 Chestnut Ridge Rd.
Montvale, NJ 07645
Wide range of quality paint
products including historical
color reproductions.
www.benjaminmoore.com

Graham Paint & Varnish
(800) 255-2628
4800 S. Richmond
Chicago, IL 60632
Their Aqua Borne brand offers a
washable flat paint with low
VOCs.
www.grahampaint.com

Masterchem Industries
(800) 325-3552
P.O. Box 368
Barnhart, MO 63012
Makers of KILZ (R) primer-seal-
er/stainblocker.
www.masterchem.com

Minwax
(800) 526-0495; (800) 462-
0194; or (800) 523-9299 (how-
to questions)
101 Prospect Avenue NW
1460 Midland Building
Cleveland, OH 44115
www.minwax.com

**Old Fashioned Milk Paint Co.,
Inc.**
(978) 448-6336
436 Main Street
Groton, MA 01450
A powdered mixture of milk pro-
tein, lime, clay and earth pigments for an authentic antique
look without hydrocarbons,
petroleum derivatives, lead, or
chemical preservatives.
www.milkpaint.com

Old Village Paints
(800) 498-7687
P.O. Box 1030
Ft. Washington, PA 19034
Line includes Colonial
Williamsburg buttermilk paint.

Sears Weatherbeater
(800) 972-4687
Sears Paint Customer Service
101 Prospect Avenue
Cleveland, OH 44115
www.sears.com

Sherwin-Williams
(800) 4-SHERWIN (474-3794)
to locate store near you; or(800)
893-0303 customer service
P.O. Box 5819
Cleveland, OH 44101-0819
Wide range of paints, stains, and
wallpapers; ask about their
EverClean washable flat latex and
authentic historical color collection.
www.sherwinwilliams.com

Wm. Zinsser & Co.
(732) 469-4367
173 Belmont Drive
Somerset, NJ 08875
Manufacturer of primers, sealers,
and other surface-prep products.
Website includes advice on
paint/wallpapering projects.
www.zinsser.com

RENOVATORS' CATALOGS, SALVAGE SHOPS, & PERIOD REPRODUCTIONS:

The Brass Light Gallery
(800) 243-9595
131 S. First Street
Milwaukee, WI 53204
www.brasslight.com

Decorators Supply Corp.
(773) 847-6300
3610 S. Morgan Street
Chicago, IL 60609
Established in 1887, this company offers traditional moldings,
capitals, and plasterwork.
www.decoratorssupply.com

Old House Interactive Network
Includes "buy/sell" listings for
everything from clawfoot tubs
and antique lumber to vintage
homes for sale.
www.oldhouse.com

Old House Journal
(202) 736-3305
One Thomas Circle NW #600
Washington, DC 20005-5811
Bi-monthly magazine for restora-
tion buffs. Publishes a yearly catalog with more than 10,000
products and services for restorers. www.oldhousejournal.com

Period Lighting Fixtures
(800) 828-6990; (413) 664-7141
167 River Road
Clarksburg, MA 01247
www.periodlighting.com

The Rebuilding Center
(503) 221-3193
2015 NW 23rd
Portland, OR 97210
A nonprofit "thrift store" for quality used building and remodeling materials.
www.rebuildingcenter.com

Rejuvenation Lamp & Fixture Co.
(888) 401-1900 to order; (888) 343-8548 lighting catalog request
2550 NW Nicolai Street
Portland, OR 97210
www.rejuvenation.com

Rejuvenation House Parts
(503) 238-1900
1100 SE Grand Avenue
Portland, OR 97214
A sister company to the Rejuvenation Lamp company, this store offers salvage architectural and hardware, plumbing, lighting, furniture, and other items for Portland area only (does not ship to other parts of the country).

Renovator's Supply
(800) 659-2211
Box 2515
Conway, NH 03818
Hundreds of antique-style kitchen and bath products including fixtures, knobs and accessories.

San Francisco Victoriana, Inc.
(415) 648-0313
2070 Newcomb Avenue
San Francisco, CA 94124
Plaster-cast corbels, ceiling medallions and other architectural details.

Van Dyke's Restorers (R)
(800) 787-3355 customer service; (800) 558-1234 to order
P.O. Box 278
Woonsocket, SD 57385
Supplies for woodworkers and antique restorers. A wide assortment of reproduction items including old-style drawer pulls, hinges, and other hardware.
www.vandykes.com/restorer.html

Vintage Wood Works
(903) 356-2158
P.O. Box 39
Quinlan, TX 75474-0039
Interior and exterior architectural details.
www.vintagewoodworks.com

PLANNING RESOURCES:

www.improvenet.com
Wide variety of remodeling information including design ideas, cost estimators, and expert advice. Their motto: "Everything you need to succeed with home improvement." Includes nationwide database of more than 600,000 contractors, architects and designers who have met certain screening requirements.

www.kitchenweb.com
Information on products plus a directory of contractors and design firms which specialize in kitchens. Offers online kitchen planner that will produce a 3-D rendering (free, but requires registration and password).

www.cmyvision.com
For techno-folks who have a scanner or digital camera, allows you to alter features using an online catalog of products such as paint, wallpaper, flooring, furniture etc. Or select a similar photo from the site to manipulate.

www.homeportfolio.com
A large selection of "premium home design products," some with online brochures. "Personal Portfolio" feature allows you to compile an online scrapbook of items.

Hearst Products
(800) 666-6421
1790 Broadway
New York, NY 10019
A source for ordering a variety of "Home Quick Planners" with reusable, peel-and-stick furniture and architectural symbols, or "3-D Home Kit" that allows you to construct a sturdy cardboard model of your home including stairs, windows, siding, and kitchen cabinets.

Family Handyman
(800) 666-3111 or (612) 854-3000
P.O. Box 5232
Harlan, IA 51593
How-to tips, home improvement library, house plans and more.
www.familyhandyman.com

Fine Homebuilding
(800) 243-7252
Taunton Press
63 S. Main Street, P.O. Box 5506
Newtown, CT 06470-5500
Beautifully done magazine written by and for professional builders offers sophisticated building tips and techniques, accompanied by lavish photo illustrations.
www.finehomebuilding.com

Home Ideas or Kitchen and Bath Ideas

Meredith Corporation
(800) 678-2872 option 5 or 9
1716 Locust Street
Des Moines, IA 50309-3023
These two Better Homes & Gardens special interest publications are available at newsstands; no subscriptions available.
www.bhglive.com

House Beautiful's Kitchens/Baths or Kitchen & Bath Planner
(800) 444-6873
The Hearst Corp.
P.O. Box 7174
Red Oak, IA 51591
www.hearstspecials.com

Renovation Style
(800) 588-4599
(a Better Homes & Gardens specialty magazine)
P.O. Box 37237
Boone, IA 50037-0237

Today's Homeowner magazine
(800) 456-6369; (212) 779-5000
Times Mirror Magazines
2 Park Avenue, 9th Floor
New York, NY 10016
10 issues/year, packed with maintenance and home improvement tips.
www.todayshomeowner.com

GOVERNMENT SOURCES & PROFESSIONAL ASSOCIATIONS:

American Institute of Architects (AIA)
(202) 626-7300
1735 New York Avenue N.W.
Washington, DC 20006
Established in 1857, the AIA currently has some 63,000 members. Check for an AIA listing in your local yellow pages (under "architects") to locate a member-architect in your area. The AIA home page (www.aiaonline.com) also provides a searchable database of architects by region.
www.aiaonline.com

American Institute of Building Design
(800) 366-2423
991 Post Road East
Westport, CT 06880
This 1500-member organization promotes the building design industry. Members who demonstrate the necessary training and qualifications (including at least 5 years of professional design experience, and submission of working drawings and letters of recommendation) are entitled to use the initials "AIBD" after their names.
A separate advanced certification program for designers is now administered by the "National Council of Building Designer Certification," entitling those who qualify to use the "certified professional building designer" designation. Approximately 600 individuals in the U.S. hold this "CPBD" credential.
www.aibd.org

American Society of Interior Designers
(800) 775-ASID (2743); (202) 546-3480
608 Massachusetts Avenue NE
Washington, DC 20002-6006
The oldest and largest professional organization for interior designers, this 30,000-plus member organization promotes professionalism and education in the field of residential and commercial interior design.
www.asid.org or
www.interiors.org (referrals)

International Interior Design Assoc.
(888) 799-IIDA (4432) or (312) 467-1950
341 Merchandise Mart
Chicago, IL 60654-1104
This 10,000-member organization promotes education and communication in the field of interior design.
www.IIDA.com

National Association of Home Builders
(800) 368-5242; (202) 822-0200
1201 - 15th Street NW
Washington, DC 20005-2800
A trade association for the housing industry, NAHB is a federation of more than 800 state and local builders' associations and boasts some 200,000 members, about one-third of which are home builders and/or remodelers. Their Remodeling Council issues certification for qualified members as "CGR" (certified graduate remodeler).
www.nahb.com

American Homeowners Foundation
(800) 489-7776; (703) 536-7776
6776 Little Falls Road
Arlington, VA 22213
This non-profit organization provides model contracts, tip sheets, and books for homeowners.
http://members.aol.com/Amerhome/amerhome

National Association of the Remodeling Industry
(703) 575-1100
4900 Seminary Road #320
Alexandria, VA 22311
Non-profit trade organization representing more than 6,000 member companies. Issues four different certifications, including "CR certified remodeler.
www.nari.org or
www.remodeltoday.com

National Kitchen & Bath Association
(800) 843-6522; (908) 852-0033
687 Willow Grove St.
Hackettstown, NJ 07840
Formerly the American Institute of Kitchen Dealers. Call for free planning kit and list of members in your area. Planning kit includes a set of Universal Design guidelines.
www.nkba.org

Home Ventilating Institute
(847) 394-0150
a division of the Air Movement & Control Assn Int'l, Inc.www.amca.org
30 W. University Drive
Arlington Hts, IL 60004-1893
A division of a nonprofit trade association, HVI tests and certifies the product performance of residential ventilating products. Offers free brochures for consumers about ventilation solutions throughout the home.

Title I Loan Program
One of HUD's most frequently used programs for financing home improvements, the Title I loan program facilitates loans of up to $25,000 for qualifying renovations to a single family home amortized over a maximum of 20 years. Though HUD insures these loans, funds actually are provided through private lenders. (A searchable list of approved lenders is available on the HUD website.)
http://www.hud.gov/progdesc/title-i.html

American Society of Home Inspectors
(800) 743-ASHI (2744); (847) 759-2835
932 Lee Street #101
Des Plaines, IL 60016
www.ashi.com

Adaptive Environments Center Inc.
(617) 695-1225
374 Congress Street #301
Boston, MA 02210
A non-profit organization formed in 1978 promoting accessibility and universal design. Publications include "A Consumer's Guide to Home Adaptation."
www.adaptenv.org

Center for Universal Design
(800) 647-6777; (919) 515-3082
North Carolina State University's School of Design
Box 8613
Raleigh, NC 27695-8613
A national research, information, and technical assistance center established in 1989, dedicated to improving the quality and availability of housing for people with disabilities.
www.design.ncsu.edu/cud

Concrete Change
(404) 378-7455
600 Dancing Fox Road
Decatur, GA 30032
An international effort to promote "visitability" in homes. Includes construction guidelines.
http://concretechange.home.mindspring.com

U.S. Access Board
(800) 872-2253; (202) 272-5434
1331 "F" Street NW, 10th Floor
Washington, D.C. 20004
The federal agency responsible for (among other things) developing standards under the Americans with Disabilities Act and Architectural Barriers Act.
www.access-board.gov

Insurance Information Institute
(800) 942-4242 (Consumer Helpline); (212) 669-9200
110 William Street
New York, NY 10038
A trade group for state insurance associations; provides brief consumer tips on preventing contractor rip-offs and information about various types of insurance.
www.iii.org

STENCILS:

Dressler Stencil Co.
(888) 656-4515
253 SW 41st Street
Renton, WA 98055-4930
www.dresslerstencils.com

MB Historic Decor (stencils)
(888) 649-1790
P.O. Box 880
Norwich, VT 05055
Reproduces the look of 18th and 19th century New England stencils.
www.CommunityInfo.com/stencils

StenArt Stencils
(856) 589-9857
P.O. Box 114
Pitman, NJ 08071
www.stenartstencils.com

Stencil Artisans League Inc.
(703) 518-4375
526 King Street #423
Alexandria, VA 22314
A non-profit international organization dedicated to the promotion and preservation of stenciling and decorative painting arts.
www.sali.org

WALLPAPER:

American Blind & Wallpaper Factory
(800) 575-8016 sales or (800) 782-5905 Customer Service
909 N. Sheldon Road
Plymouth, MI 48170
www.abwf.com

Imperial Wallcoverings
(800) 539-5399
23645 Mercantile Road
Cleveland, OH 44122
www.imp-wall.com

National Blind & Wallpaper Factory
(800) 477-8000
400 Galleria
Southfield, MI 48034
www.nationaldecorating.com

www.villagehome.com
Searchable source for wallpapers, borders and fabrics; offers tips on buying and hanging wallpaper.

York Wallcoverings
(800) 375-9675
750 Linden Avenue
York, PA 17405

WINDOWS, DOORS, & SKYLIGHTS:

Andersen Windows
(800) 426-4261
100 4th Avenue N
Bayport, MN 55003-1096
www.andersenwindows.com

Caradco Window Company
(800) 238-1866
P.O. Box 920
Rantoul, IL 61866
www.caradco.com

CertainTeed Corporation
(800) 782-8777 or (610) 341-7000
P.O. Box 860
750 E. Swedesford Road
Valley Forge, PA 19482
www.certainteed.com

Hurd Millwork Co.
(800) 2BE-HURD (223-4873)
575 S. Whelen Ave.
Medford, WI 54451-0319
www.hurd.com

Marvin Windows & Doors
(800) 346-5128
P.O. Box 100
Warroad, MN 56763
www.marvin.com

Milgard Windows
(800) 391-6937 OR (800) MILGARD for dealer near you
965- 54th Ave East
Box 11368
Tacoma, WA 98411-0368
www.milgard.com

National Fenestration Rating Council (NFRC)
(301) 589-6372
1300 Spring Street #500
Silver Spring, MD 20910
www.nfrc.org

Window & Door Manufacturers Assn.
(800) 223-2301; (847) 299-5200
1400 E. Touhy Avenue #470
Des Plaines, IL 60018-3305
Formerly the "National Wood Window & Door Association," this trade organization represents approximately 130 U.S. and Canadian window/door manufacturers and suppliers, and certifies products made in accordance with WDMA standards. How-to guides and other informational literature available for a nominal fee.www.wdma.com

Owens Corning
(800) GET PINK (438-7465)
1 Owens Corning Pkwy
Toledo, OH 43659
www.owenscorning.com

Peachtree Doors & Windows
(800) 252-4720 customer service or (888) 888-3814 consumer service
2774 Ramsey Road
Gainesville, GA 30501
www.peachtreedoors.com
Pella Corporation
(800) 54-PELLA (547-3552)
102 Main Street
Pella, IA 50219
www.pella.com

Pozzi Wood Windows
(800) 257-WOOD (-9663)
62845 Boyd Acres Rd.
Bend, OR 97708
www.pozzi.com

Solatube International, Inc.
(800) 966-7652 for information;
(888) 476-5288 for technical
info.
2210 Oak Ridge Way
Vista, CA 92083
www.solatube.com

Sun Pipe Co., Inc.
(800) 844-4786 for dealer near
you; (847) 272-6977
P.O. Box 2223
Northbrook, IL 60065
www.sunpipe.com

SunScope
(800) 449-0644
Sky-Tech Industries, Inc.
9135-39 Avenue
Edmonton, Alberta CANADA
T6E-5Y2
www.sunscope.com

Sun Tunnel
(800) 369-3664 or (408) 369-7447
786 McGlincy Lane
Campbell, CA 95008
www.suntunnel.com

Velux-America
(800) 283-2831
Box 5001
Greenwood, SC 29648-5001
www.velux.com or
www.velux-america.com

Weather Shield Manufacturing, Inc.
(800) 477-6808
P.O. Box 309
531 N. 8th Street
Medford, WI 54451
www.weathershield.com